DE CONTROVERSIIS CHRISTIANAE FIDEI ADVERSUS HUIUS TEMPORIS HAERETICOS

ON THE CONTROVERSIES OF THE CHRISTIAN FAITH AGAINST THE HERETICS OF THIS TIME

ST. ROBERT BELLARMINE
OF THE SOCIETY OF JESUS
DOCTOR OF THE CHURCH

TRANSLATED FROM
THE ORIGINAL LATIN BY

RYAN GRANT

MEDIATRIX PRESS

ON THE CANONIZATION
AND
VENERATION OF THE SAINTS

by
ST. ROBERT BELLARMINE, S.J.
Doctor of the Church

Translated by
Ryan Grant

MEDIATRIX PRESS

MMXIX

ISBN: 978-1-953746-17-7

Translated from: *De Controversiis Christianae Fidei*, tomus 2, 1721, Prague.

©Ryan Grant, 2019, all rights reserved.

Layout and typography © Mediatrix Press. No part of this work may be reproduced in either physical or electronic format, except for quotations in reviews, journals or classroom use without the express permission of the publisher.

Cover art:
Madonna Enthroned with all the Saints
-Peter Paul Rubens
St. Augustinuskerk, Antwerp

Mediatrix Press
607 E. 6th Ave.
Post Falls, ID 83854
www.mediatrixpress.com

Table of Contents

Translator's Preface ix

Preface 1

CHAPTER I
    The arguments of the heretics, with which they attempt to prove that the saints are not yet blessed, etc. 19

CHAPTER II
    We prove from the testimony of the Church that the souls of the saints already enjoy the vision of God. 31

CHAPTER III
    The same is proven by the testimony of the Scriptures. 35

CHAPTER IV
    The same truth is confirmed by the Greek Fathers. 51

CHAPTER V
    The same is proven from the testimonies of the Latin Fathers 65

CHAPTER VI
    The same is proven from arguments that, although taken from reason nevertheless, have their foundation in the Scriptures. 81

CHAPTER VII
    The Church rightly canonizes saints. 89

CHAPTER VIII
    Whose office it is to canonize the saints........ 93

CHAPTER IX
    It must be believed that the Pope cannot err in the canonization of Saints 97

CHAPTER X
    Uncanonized saints may be venerated privately, but not publicly............................ 101

CHAPTER XI
    A question is proposed on the cult of the saints, with the arguments of our adversaries. 103

CHAPTER XII
    The Catholic teaching is explained........... 107

CHAPTER XIII
    The Catholic teaching is asserted by argumentation. 115

CHAPTER XIV
    The arguments proposed previously are answered. 127

CHAPTER XV
    The controversy on the invocation of the saints is proposed. 133

CHAPTER XVI
    Some frauds and lies of the heretics are detected 135

CHAPTER XVII
    How the saints must not be invoked 139

CHAPTER XVIII
The saints pray for us. 143

CHAPTER XIX
The Saints must be invoked 153

CHAPTER XX
The arguments of our adversaries are answered
. . . . 169

Translator's Preface

ST. ROBERT BELLARMINE'S work in defense of the saints, their place in heaven, their canonization and veneration, etc., ranks, like all of his works, among the classical works of Catholic theology. As the father apologetics as we know it, his martialing of scriptural exegesis and patristic testimony is second to none.

One of the most visible effects of the Reformation in every country where it took hold was the marked iconoclasm realized in the destruction of statues, images, works of art and the banning of pilgrimages. Often times the early Protestants would cut the heads off of the images but allow the rest to remain as a sign that we no longer commit "idolatry". Otherwise, churches were gutted and white-washed, and turned into buildings for secular business. The basis was that Scripture does not countenance the veneration of saints and to do so is to worship them like new idols.

Thus, Bellarmine meets the attack right on the Protestants' own ground in a manner that will be familiar to those who have read other works of Bellarmine which we have brought into translation. First Scripture, and an exegesis of the passage accompanied by the testimonies of the Fathers; then the testimonies of the Fathers in general, and lastly arguments from reason. Additionally, Bellarmine uses the universal witness of the Church as seen in ancient times in an unbroken testimony to the present, as a sign of the guidance of the Holy Spirit throughout the life of the Church.

Nevertheless, as text criticism of patristic sources was still in its beginnings in the 16th century, sometimes texts were improperly attributed. Bellarmine himself engages in this text criticism at times, when it seemed clear to him that a given Father could not have authored a certain book. Other times, he cites sources that subsequently were deemed by scholars to not have been written by that author. We have endeavored to note this whenever possible in a footnote.

Moreover, the original Latin furnished a great difficulty with the translation into English. The word *colere*, which generically means to worship with respect to religion, is used by Catholic writers both in reference to God as well as to the saints, but with the distinction of with *latria* (adoration) and *dulia* (veneration). It seemed that on the one hand, to be faithful to the Latin and avoid difficulties when both are objects of the verb *colere*, it would be better to use "worship" in regard to the saints. Unfortunately, this is too jarring in modern English, which has moved beyond the notion of worship in regard to anything other than God. For some time, Catholic writers in English have adopted the word "veneration" in regard to the saints because worship now means *latria*. Where the two run together we have placed footnotes to aid the reader. Rather more on account of this fact, the Protestant critic would be able to quote Bellarmine without recourse to the distinctions of *latria* and *dulia* (which they reject) and say "Lo! Did we not say papists worship the saints!" Thus we have been forced to depart from the literal meaning of the word to accommodate the exigencies of modern English.

The English reader will also see the word "cult", which is now pejorative in modern English. The Latin word *cultus* merely refers to worship or veneration conferred religiously, and its value is determined by context. As a technical term, it could not be suitably changed to suit the tone of modern English.

Translator's Preface

Lastly, I want to thank above all my lovely wife, whose support has been essential to continue these works. Also, Ben Douglass and Ashton Wilkins, who assisted in the editing of the work and provided many useful suggestions. Then, all of the benefactors of the Bellarmine Translation Project, whose donations got this project off the ground to begin with, and without whom it should never have happened.

We hope that the publication of this, and all of our forthcoming translations of St. Robert Bellarmine's works will also benefit Catholic theology and assist in recouping the Catholic tradition.

Post Falls, ID
2019

Preface

ON THE CHURCH TRIUMPHANT
or

On the Glory and cult of the Saints

AT LENGTH, we have come to elucidate with our disputation that part of the Catholic Church which enjoys the eternal *aevum* in blessed heaven with Christ the King, as well as to defend it against both the arguments as well as the lies and calumnies of the heretics. Truly, these blessed souls of holy angels and men do not require human defense and assistance, since they dwell in the highest halls and are most safe from any enemy, daily leading new triumphs and (as St. Cyprian says) altogether secure in their own happiness. Nevertheless, it is useful for us and, to speak more truly, necessary by many accounts, that the glory of the Saints upon which the heretics try to heap up and pour out insults, be known and respected through all the world and altogether vindicated, freed and resplendent from the fog of all idolatry.

Nevertheless, we have not established a panegyric speech on the praises of the saints; rather, we merely give the opening remarks to the coming disputation with this little preface. Thus, I will only speak on a few of the sophistries, lies and abuse of the heretics against the saints, those which lay up a great impediment to curing the great insanity of the heretics themselves. Those lies which not only would despoil the Church of their characteristic patronage, but will also bring about the most dread and just wrath of the Divine upon all mortal men.

Still, there are many things about which we and the heretics of our time dispute; there are many things in our Church that they rebuke, such as church buildings, monasteries, academies, dogmas, rites, and at length, men of every order; they lack many things, they despoil many things, they clamor for many things to be emended and corrected; but there is nothing which they are terrified of and hate more than the invocation of the saints, the cult of relics and the veneration of images. For, they would have it that these three things contain manifest impiety and idolatry. By this one thing, they wish to provide cover for their separation from us, namely their impious separation and defection from the Catholic Church. In this name alone do they defend their thievery, sacrileges in churches, sacking of churches, breaking of images, slaughter of priests, and profanations of all sacred things because they claim they are making war for piety against idols. For this very reason they declare the most just censure of the Church and the pastoral staffs of Bishops (whereby in the meantime their fury is repressed or delayed), an impious persecution as if it were roused against God on behalf of idols. At length, they hold the provinces and nations that they have deceived bound and tightly netted by these chains and fetters.

For, in this way they have persuaded peoples that we hold dead men for the living God, worship bones, ashes, wood and stone in place of the supreme and eternal spirit, and this pernicious persuasion has penetrated their minds to such an extent that we labor in not only an unjust but even grave and long lasting infamy. And although, sometimes they may hear many things from the gravity,

Author's Preface

wisdom, justice, and kindness of our own, *i.e.* Catholic men, on the zeal for preaching, on moderation in all things, nevertheless, they cannot but turn away from sermons of this sort when they remember to whom so many outstanding praises are given by our preachers, and conclude that they are all just the same as idolaters that adore the spirits of the dead, cadavers, pictures and statues.

Furthermore, to gain more trust and so that nobody thinks I am imagining something for the sake of a rhetorical gloss, I will relate a few things from their books so that we will have their very own works as heralds and witnesses of their impiety. First, Luther, the leader and prince of every sect, in his sermon which he published on the Cross, declares, as if from a tribunal: "Because the relics of the saints are nothing other than seductions of the faithful, it would please God for all relics of this sort to be hidden away deep within the earth lest the people would worship strange gods."

So Luther would have it that the memory of all the Apostles and martyrs, to say nothing of the other saints, should be obliterated from memory. Later, he says the same thing while preaching on the Gospel of the Lord's Annunciation: "Papists constitute the Virgin Mary as God, and attribute to her omnipotence in heaven and on earth," and again: "In popery all present themselves to Mary and expect more favor and grace from her than Christ himself."

Thereafter, Philip Melanchthon, an offshoot of Luther and an outstanding disciple, when he commented on the first precept of the Decalogue in *Locis Communibus*, and made a distinction between a certain degree of sinners and us, as he himself said, he would join papists with infidels. He was content to do so for this one reason: that it is the same thing to make many gods and to invoke dead saints;

nor are invocation of the saints and the cult of statues different from heathen customs.

Moreover, the Lutheran Centuriators of Magdeburg, near the end of their writing on the first *Century*, posited that the foundations of Catholic doctrine in regard to the invocation and veneration of the Blessed Virgin Mary as well as the other saints was never approved by the Apostles in word or example, but rather was everywhere condemned and forbidden as idolatry; thence, after these things in *Singulis Centuriis*, they warn, cry out, repeat, and drive home nothing more often than that we have no Church because we have defected from the one true God to a multitude of false gods and mute simulacra. But in the preface for the *Sixth Century*, they quite seriously, precisely and tragically deplore the state, or rather the fall and ruin of the Church. They suppose that it began with a defect in the second and third century that grew worse in the fourth and fifth century, and at length gave way in the sixth and was altogether corrupted and collapsed. In this way they preach on the cause of so grave a destruction:

"In the first place, this horrible and pernicious darkness in the very body of doctors, arose like dark clouds seizing the whole heaven, because some of the very Doctors of the Church and other superstitious men everywhere increased ceremonies and human cults in churches. For sacred buildings began to be built in all places with vast expenses, altogether pagan in custom; not principally for the purpose of handing down the Word of God in those places, but that some would show honor to the relics of the saints, and there, stupid men venerated the dead. And how eloquent was that Gregory, now called 'great', how ardent, when he drew up a method for consecrating these temples from a tripod. ... On that occasion dead creatures, as well as

Author's Preface

bloodless and half-rotten bones began to be worshiped, invoked, fastened with divine honor and prayers in those very places. The doctors of the Church not only connived in these things, but also but also helped them. Therefore, a calamity of this sort and the destruction of the estate of Christ, in the very Church was willed into being and passed down by those who were especially the watchman and sentries of the Church."

Moving on, John Calvin, after many very serious debates with his own dragged the greater part of Lutherans into his net, although he did not obtain some kingdom among the pastors of Luther. In a book which he wrote on the need to reform the Church to the Emperor Charles V, he said that the greatest reason for dissension between them and us is the fact that his party, *i.e.* all the sects of this time, worship one God, but ours, namely Catholics, so distributed the offices of God among the saints that they add them to the supreme God as colleagues, and God is hidden in the crowd. And they not only worship the saints in place of God but even their bones, clothing, shoes and simulacra. In his book *The Institutes* (lib. 4 cap. 21), he reviews the reasons why they made their break with us, and he places as the first one that they can have no accord with us whereby they would not be polluted by open idolatry. The extent to which he says that idolatry flourishes with us can be seen from book 3, ch. 20, where speaking on the invocation of the saints he says: "Then individuals adopted particular saints, and put their faith in them, just as if they had been tutelary deities. And thus not only were gods set up according to the number of the cities (the charge which the prophet brought against Israel of old, Jer. 2:28; 11:13), but according to the number of individuals."

St. Robert Bellarmine

I once met with a man from the school of Calvin whom I questioned, since he was otherwise very civil with me, so that I might recall him from that insanity. I began to ask what the Calvinists most rebuked in our doctrines and what especially displeased them. Then at length, what was the particular reason why they had separated themselves from communion with the Church, from obedience to their bishops, from the rest of the body of the faithful, from the footsteps of their forefathers with such a manifest danger to their eternal salvation? He answered that the particular cause was that we invoke the saints in prayers, and that we attribute divinity to dead men. But these shams are most impudent lies. For what Catholic ever equated sacred images, the blessed pledges of the saints, the martyrs, the Apostles, or even the souls of angels, or the very queen of heaven, Mary the mother of God, with the one true God?

Who in the Catholic Church offered the sacrifice due to the one God to saints, or relics or images? Do we not, by this one outward sign, even if there were no other, testify clearly enough that we also in mind and thought embrace one God and serve him only with his own peculiar worship? Do we not clearly distinguish between that honor which is due to God alone, and that veneration which is piously and religiously granted to the friends of God and other sacred things on account of God himself? But, although those are lies and calumnies (as we said), in the meantime, because of these very lies innumerable peoples, kingdoms, nations, and many thousands of souls redeemed by the blood of Christ have been separated from the body of Christ and, as branches wrested from a tree by the force of a storm, are strewn about, and like sheep that wander from the fold without the protection of any

Author's Preface

shepherds or dogs, they wander in the mountains and are daily made prey to the wolves.

But since we have said something about lies and calumnies, abuses and insults, another thing will also need to be said. In the books and conduct of the heretics there is so much contempt for all the saints, and such horrible blasphemies against all heavenly things, that I am astonished at the patience of the divine majesty. For, I will omit the fact that the Calvinists have raged against sacred images with such furor, that in many places they either completely destroy them or bury them in mud and filth, or destroy the eyes, noses, and ears; I will say nothing of the fact that the very sign of the cross, revered by the Angels, terrifying to the demons, salutary to the human race, they everywhere throw down, spit upon and trample on. I might also pass over the fact that the blessed bodies of the Saints which the piety of our fathers enclosed in cases of gold and silver, since they had been dwellings and instruments of the Holy Spirit, such that God had embellished them with signs and miracles, were dug up by the Calvinists from the altars they had overturned, consigned to the flames and cast into rivers. So that I shall omit all these things, and only speak to the insulting words, I shall say: What, I ask, of Erasmus of Rotterdam? Did he not, after a long interval, surpass the impiety of Lucian? For Lucian ridiculed false and truly ridiculous gods; but this new Lucian treated the countrymen of the angels and the friends of the true God (as the Apostle calls them) contumeliously.

In a colloquy titled *Naufragium*, he introduced a certain man asking the other if he would implore the assistance of some saint under the threatening danger of death? He responded: "Not even that. Why should I bother? Heaven is so spacious, if I were to commend my soul to one of the saints, say to Peter, because perhaps he will hear me sooner since he is present at the gate, then before he meets with God and before I might explain the cause I will have already perished." These are the witty, or rather sacrilegious jokes of Erasmus. Also in the same book, altogether by the custom of Lucian, he substituted Venus for the Blessed Virgin Mary in the command of the sea, and what Christian would dare to compare the latter, a Virgin, whom St. John Chrysostom so truly wrote is holier and more pure than the seraphic spirits, with the former, a most impure harlot?

Moreover, in his dialogue *de peregrinatione religionis*, was he was not embarrassed to publish a fictional letter in the name of the Virgin Mary in which the very Mother of truth is introduced as being the author of the false dogmas of Luther? Thus that fictional Mary writes to Glaucoplutus:

"Following Luther you strenuously persuade men of the fact that it is worthless to invoke the saints, and know from me that what you have undertaken is good and a great favor since hitherto I have only barely not been worn out by the woeful weeping of mortals. Everything is sought from one woman as if my Son were always an infant because he is contrived and painted as such in my bosom." But I am disgusted and ashamed to relate such things, which nevertheless abound in the overwrought books of Erasmus.

Moreover, Martin Luther, in his sermon on the birth of the Blessed Virgin, made so much of the patronage of the Mother of God that he did not hesitate to declare boldly, that he no more esteemed the prayers of the Blessed Virgin Mary than those of any person whatsoever: because we are

Author's Preface

all equally holy and just, even the Virgin Mary, and the rest of the saints, no matter how great.

So, let Bernard stop enumerating the prerogatives of Mary; let Chrysostom no longer say the Virgin Mother of God is more honorable than the Cherubim and without compare more glorious than the Seraphim; let not the voice of Anselm be heard hereafter saying that Mary shines with a purity so splendid that, apart from God, none greater can be conceived; for we are all equally just and holy as the Virgin Mary herself. It profited Mary nothing that she raised the first monument of virginity, that as a Virgin she conceived God, gave birth to God, reared him; that she was the companion of all his journeys, labors, toils and troubles, following him even to the cross when his disciples fled, and finally accepted a most bitter martyrdom, a sword of sorrow piercing her heart. For without so many labors we are all equally just and holy as the Virgin herself. And Peter and Paul, as well as the rest of the Apostles, traveled for no reason to disseminate the Gospel through the whole world with such labor; in vain did they shed their blood as martyrs for Christ; thus the vigils, fasts, cares, prostrations, coarse sackcloth and incessant battles with demons of the holy hermits were empty, because without so many labors and without so much sweat, Lutherans, resting at home in the bosom and embrace of their wife with the best food and drink steal heaven, and are equally as holy and just as the Virgin Mary and the rest of the saints, no matter how great.

Now, let us come to the Centuriators; for they are most outstanding and religious historians who, in the earlier part of their book *on the First Century*, while they explain the life of Christ, would have it that when the Blessed Virgin Mary lost her son in the temple, she sinned so gravely that they do not hesitate to compare it with the first and most severe sin of Eve. They do not even fear to ask or be uncertain as to whether it might also be more severe. Later in the same book, they attribute fifteen falls and errors to Peter the prince of the Apostles, some of which, they teach, are most worthy of eternal tortures. Not much later they rebuke the Apostle Paul because in Asia was weighed down for a while and despaired of life, and that in favor of James he observed Jewish ceremonies in Jerusalem, and by that fact he confirmed the Jews even more in error than he helped his weak brethren. Yet, in the *third Century*, and all the following ones, to the end of the fourth chapter, they accuse all the Fathers not only for holding inconvenient opinions and blemishes, but also of introducing into the Church errors, doctrines of straw and smoke by their writings, to such an extent that were it not for Luther bearing again the torch of doctrine to us and scattering the tempestuous fog, even now we would all be blind and deprived of life.

What shall we say about that impure and blasphemous Quintinus, the father of the libertines in France who, on Calvin's authority (*in instructione contra Libertinos*, c. 9) so petulantly raged against all the saints that he called Paul a broken vessel, John a stupid youth, Matthew a usurer and Peter a denier of Christ?

Then Calvin, who so severely convicts others of impiety, was himself so pious and religious that he was not content with the insults with which he troubles all the saints who lived after the coming of Christ, he also extended to those who preceded the coming of the same savior by many centuries the whip of his tongue. So in the *Institutes*, book 3 ch. 2 §31, he makes Abraham the worshipper of idols; he says that Sarah sinned in many

Author's Preface

ways when she placed a maidservant under her husband (lib. 3 cap. 2 § 31); that Rebecca corrupted the truth of God with different frauds and deceits, when she procured with a wicked plan the blessing of her son, deceived her husband and compelled Jacob to lie. He rebukes Judas Maccabeus (lib. 3 cap. 5 § 8) for superstition. He rebukes his preposterous zeal whereby he commanded sacrifice to be offered for the dead. He teaches that Sephora was a stupid woman and sinned gravely because she circumcised her son (lib. 4 c. 15 § 20). Even Moses himself, in chapter 32 of Exodus, whereby old age had nothing sweeter, wiser or holier, Calvin accuses of arrogance and pride because he prescribed the law of God imperiously and deprived it of its justice.

Moreover, first he scurrilously talks nonsense about the holy men of the New Testament, saying that if they should hear the prayers of mortals then their ears should be so long that they extend from heaven to earth. Then, by the same contemptuous speech, he names dead men shadows, demons, and even sewage (*Instit.* lib. 3 c. 20 § 27). But in the book which he titled *De vera Ecclesia reformandae ratione*, he also called them monsters, murderers, and beasts; scarcely ever were greater blasphemies devised! And why? If a Catholic were to call not Calvin himself, but his wife (for with them it is unlawful to be made a bishop unless he is at least a man of one wife), nay more his children or friends or even his servants and maidservants, demons, shadows, sewage, beasts, monsters, murderers, etc., how well would Calvin take it? Wouldn't he think a great injury had been done to him? Would he not take it ill? And equally, how will Christ take it when his friends, members of his household, sons and most beloved whom he himself has deigned to give such honor in heaven, as it says in the Apocalypse: "If anyone conquers I will give to him to sit on my throne, just as I conquered and sat in the throne of my Father", I say, those sublime princes, consorts of the kingdom and divine thrones are named shadows, devils, and sewage by some rather arrogant worm of the earth? God will certainly not take it with equanimity, but will at length afflict blasphemers and profaners of this sort with eternal punishments.

But we, if we are countrymen of the saints, if we have any zeal for the faith, let us be roused and enkindled as is fitting, moved with pious and religious indignation, so as to resist bitterly nefarious men. Let the Lutherans imitate their fathers, Porphyry, Julian, Vigilantius, Wycliffe, and as many as ever waged impious war with the heavenly saints and, as in the fables of the poets about giants, willed to cast them down and drag them from their heavenly seats. But let us hold fast to the footsteps of our fathers, Athanasius, Ambrose, Jerome, Paulinus, Augustine, and Gregory. He that religiously emulates the glory of the Apostles and Martyrs, upholds their deeds against detractors with all their strength in argument, will always be zealous to nourish that memory with sermons, honor it with basilicas, celebrate it with songs, propagate it with letters, and consecrate it to eternity. So it will happen that those who imitate the crimes of the ancient heretics are joined with the latter in a communion of punishment, while we, who followed our leaders in this devotion to virtue, will have the same rewards and crowns as our fiends. Now let us approach more nearly to the matter.

Author's Preface

Order of Disputation

This disputation is contained in twelve particular questions. The *first* is on the beatitude of the saints: whether the souls of the saints see God and are truly blessed before the day of judgment? This question is the foundation of all others, for on that account, before the coming of Christ the spirits of the Patriarchs and Prophets were not so worshiped, nor invoked in the way that we now worship the Apostles and Martyrs as well as invoke them, because at that time they were still detained in infernal prisons.

Second, on canonization which follow in order from the first disputation on beatitude. For after we will have learned that the holy men enjoy life with God and reign with him as blessed, we will need to learn who they are, and that we cannot know certainly by any means except the public testimony of the Church, which we now call canonization.

Third, on cult, where it is established who they are, who are to be numbered among the spirits of the blessed; then the question follows as to whether they must be adored with any sort of adoration.

Fourth, on invocation, which is the most excellent kind of adoration.

Fifth, on the relics of the saints, whether not only the spirits of the saints, but even their bodies, or bones, ashes, and other relics of this sort may be venerated.

Sixth, on images, whether they may be venerated, and with what kind of cult.

St. Robert Bellarmine

Seventh – twelfth, on those things by which due reverence is shown not only to some saints but also to the whole of the heavenly Jerusalem by the Church, which makes its pilgrimage on earth, *i.e.* on basilicas, pilgrimages, vows, vigils, fasting and feasts.[1]

---

[1] The fifth through twelfth disputations on relics, images, Churches, etc. will appear in a subsequent volume.

Dedicated with Grateful Affection to:

JESSE BONDERMAN

Whose financial support has made this work possible.

On Beatitude, the Canonization and Invocation of the Saints

CHAPTER I
The Arguments of the Heretics, with which they Attempt to Prove that the Saints Are not yet Blessed, etc.

THEREFORE, the first question is: *Whether the spirits of pious men who are freed from the body and need no purgation, have already been admitted to enjoy eternal beatitude which is in the glorious vision of God?*

It was an opinion of the ancient and recent heretics that all souls of any holy men you like, are preserved in certain hidden receptacles until the day of the last judgment, where they neither see God nor can be called blessed except in hope.

The first of the heretics that asserted this, as far back as I could go from the authors I gathered, was Tertullian. He taught: "That region, I say the bosom of Abraham, is not heaven, still it is higher than hell, and it offers rest to the souls of the just until the consummation of all things shall pluck them out through the resurrection of all in the fullness of mercy; then it appears from the heavenly promise, which Marcion claimed for his own as if it were not promulgated by the creator." (*In Marcionem*, lib. 4). He also holds that in his book *De Anima* in the last two chapters.

Vigilantius followed him, as we see him cited by Jerome (*Contra Vigilantium*), "You say that the souls of the Apostles and Martyrs sit either in the bosom of Abraham, or in the place of rest, or under the altar of God, nor can they be present in their tombs and where they will, namely they are of the senatorial dignity that they are not among murderers in the foulest prison, but in free and honest safety, in islands of misfortune and are closed in the fields of Elysium."

St. Robert Bellarmine

Guido[1] attributes the same error to the Armenians in *summa de haereticis*. The Greeks persisted in the same error, which is clear both from the Council of Florence (sess. 1) and St. Thomas Aquinas (*in opusculo* 6, cap. 9). Luther holds the same error in *praelect. in Genesin*, as Frederick Staphylus shows (*Epitome trimembri Lutheranae Theologiae*, par. 2). Cornelius Agrippa holds the same thing (*de occulta Philosophia*, lib. 3).

John Calvin also holds the same error, for in book 4 of the *Institutes*, c. 20 § 20, he says that only Christ entered the sanctuary of heaven, but all the rest reside in the atrium, and there await even to the consummation of the world. And in §24 he says the souls of the Saints are still joined in the same faith and charity with us. Where there is faith, there certainly is no vision. And in chapter 25, §6, he says: "Wouldn't only a rash fool inquire in what place the souls of the just are, or whether they enjoy glory or not? Meanwhile, since Scripture everywhere bids us to depend upon the expectation of the arrival of Christ, and delays the glory and the crown until a later time, we are content with the prescribed boundaries of divinity, and concede the souls that died in labor for the pious militia are in a blessed rest where, with happy joy, they await the fruition of the promised glory," etc. Note the wondrous stupidity of the man, who says it is stupid and rash to even ask whether the souls of the just enjoy glory while at the same time, he still boldly defines that they do not yet enjoy glory, but await it. Calvin advances no arguments for his view, but there are many difficult ones, some which the

---

[1] Guido Terreni de Perpiniano, O.Carm, 1260-1342. He was a Catalan philosopher and theologian at the University of Paris, and one of the most outstanding figures of the medieval Carmelite ordre.

Ch. I: The Arguments of the Heretics

Greeks usually advance, and others that usually advance them on their behalf.

1) The *first* argument is taken from the decree of John XXII, who is related to have declared this and commanded the Parisians not to teach otherwise either in schools or Churches, and they should promote no man to degrees in theology unless he would first swear that he would defend this opinion. William of Ockham is a witness of this affair in his work *on 93 days*; John Gerson in serm. *de Pascha*, and Marsilius of Padua in *4 sent.* qu. 13, art. 3, as well as Adrian (*in 4*) where he disputes on the Sacrament of Confirmation.

2) The *second* argument is taken from the Scriptures. 1) In Matthew 20:8, where the householder rendered the wage to the workers at the same time in the evening; moreover, it is certain that the resurrection is understood by the evening, and eternal life by the farthing. 2) Hebrews 11:39, "All these being approved by the testimony of faith, received not the promise; God providing some better thing for us, that they should not be perfected without us." 3) 1 John 3:2, "We know that when he will appear (Christ in his second coming), we will be alike, because we will see him as he is." 4) Apocalypse 6:9, "I saw under the altar the souls of them that were slain for the word of God." What does it mean by "those hidden under the altar", except some refashioned receptacle, where the souls live in rest, although in darkness?

3) The *third* argument is taken from the testimonies of the Greek Fathers. St. Justin Martyr in quest. 60 from those which the nations posed to Christians, says the story in the Gospel on the rich man and Lazarus is not true history, and when giving the reason says: "Before the resurrection, reward is not rendered to anyone for what they did in life." And in quest. 76, he says: "If there are no rewards for

works before the resurrection, was there some fruit to the thief when his soul was introduced into paradise? It is answered, the thief attained membership in the body of the just and saw himself, and those things which were below him, and in addition, both the angels and demons.

Irenaeus, (book 5, ch. 31), says: "For as the Lord went away in the midst of the shadow of death, where the souls of the dead were, yet afterwards arose in the body, and after the resurrection was taken up [into heaven], it is manifest that the souls of His disciples also, upon whose account the Lord underwent these things, shall go away into the invisible place allotted to them by God, and there remain until the resurrection, awaiting that event; then receiving their bodies, and rising in their entirety, that is bodily, just as the Lord arose, they shall come thus into the presence of God."

Origen (*hom. 7 in Leviticus*), says: "The saints have not yet received their joy, nor the Apostles, but they await, that 'I may be made a partaker of their joy'." And in book 2 *Periarchon*, near the end, he says that the saints after death are detained in an earthly paradise and hence they, who are more pure, rise up to the places of the air.

Chrysostom (*in hom. 39 in 1 Corinthians*) on 1 Corinthians 15:19, *If in this life we only have hope in Christ, we are of all men most miserable*, says: "What do you say, O Paul? How *in this life only have we hope*, if our bodies be not raised, the soul abiding and being immortal? Because even if the soul abide, even if it be infinitely immortal, as indeed it is, without the flesh it shall not receive those hidden good things, as neither truly shall it be punished. For all things shall be made manifest before the judgment-seat of Christ, *that every one may receive the things done in the body, according to that he hath done, whether it be good*

Ch. I: The Arguments of the Heretics

or bad. (2 Cor. v. 10.) Therefore he says, *if in this life only we have hope in Christ, we are of all men most pitiable.* For if the body rise not again, the soul abides uncrowned without that blessedness which is in heaven."

He says the same thing in *homily 28 on the epistle to the Hebrews*: "Lest they might seem to have the advantage over us by being crowned before us, he appointed one time of crowning for all; and he that gained the victory so many years before will receive his crown with you."

Theodoret, commenting on Hebrews 11, says: "The struggles of the saints were so many and so great, yet they have not yet received their crowns." Theophylactus, commenting on the same passage, says; "The saints have as yet attained nothing of the heavenly promises." And in chapter 16 of Luke, he teaches that the story about Lazarus is a parable, not history, because the goods and evils have not yet been distributed to the just and unjust. Oecumenius, commenting on the same passage, says: "All the saints merited testimony that they pleased God through faith, but they have not yet attained the goods promised to the just."

Arethas, the Bishop of Caesarea, says on chapter 6 of the Apocalypse: "By their hope, which they contemplate through understanding as if in a mirror, they are duly freed from all foolishness and rejoice, resting in the bosom of Abraham. For it was said to many saints, every husbandman of virtue is worthy of a place, from where he attains a certain understanding about his future glory."

Euthymius, commenting on chapter 16 of Luke, says that the story of Lazarus and the rich man is a parable, whereby something will be appointed after the day of judgment. And on chapter 23, he says: "And then he gave to him preservation in paradise just as a pledge of his kingdom, which is the fruition of ineffable and eternal goods, which no eye has seen, etc."

This argument is confirmed because the Greek fathers simply deny that God can be seen by a creature; therefore, they ought to deny much more that he is seen before the day of judgment. See Chrysostom in *hom. 23 on Genesis*, where he says that God is not even visible to the angels. Likewise, homily 14 *on John*, where he says the angels never saw the son of God until after the incarnation. Theodoret holds similar things in his Dialogue *Immutabilis*. Theophylactus on that of John 1, *No man has ever seen God*, and Euthymius on the same passage. On that passage one can add from the Latins Jerome, as Augustine witnesses in *Epistle 111 ad Fortunatianum*.

4) The *fourth* Argument is taken from the testimonies of the Latin Fathers. Lactantius (lib. 7 cap. 21) says: "Let nobody think that souls are judged right away after death, for all are detained in one and common custody until the time shall arrive in which the greatest judge shall make an examination of their merits."

Victorinus the Martyr, on chapter 6 of the Apocalypse says: "Moreover, he says the souls of the slain see themselves under the altar, that is under the earth. ... In the end of time the perpetual reward will come to the saints, and perpetual damnation to the impious."

Hilary on that verse in Psalm 138:8, *If I descend into hell, you are there*, says: "This is the law of human necessity, that souls descend from buried bodies into hell." And lest one might think he speaks about the souls of the impious, he adds: "Such a law the Lord does not reject to the preservation of the true man, etc." Therefore he means to say, it is so necessary that the souls are in hell while the

Ch. I: The Arguments of the Heretics

flesh is in the tomb that even the Lord willed them to undergo the law.

Prudentius, in a hymn on the funeral rites of the dead, teaches that holy souls depart this life in earthly paradise, or in the bosom of Abraham, which that rich man, burning, caught sight of from afar:

> What paradise are thou supplying,
> Where pure souls can find a fair land?
> In the bosom with just Eleazar,
> Of the holy old man they shall lie;
> While the rich man, an agonized gazer,
> For the flowers of God's garden shall sigh.
> Redeemer, we follow Thy saying,
> When conquering dark death in Thy strife,
> Thou badest the thief, to Thee praying
> To tread in Thy footsteps to life.
> Lo! Now to the faithful victorious,
> The bright road to Paradise runs,
> We enter the glorious paradise,
> The serpent once closed to God's sons.[1]

---

[1] Quanam regione jubebis
Animam requiescere puram?
Gremio senis abdita sancti
Recubabit, ut est Eleazar,
Quem floribus undique septum
Dives procul aspicit ardens.
Patet ecce fidelibus ampli
Via lucida jam paradisi,
Licet, et nemus illud adire
Homini, quod ademerat anguis.
In *Exsequiis.*

St. Robert Bellarmine

St. Ambrose (lib. 2 *de Cain*, cap. 2) says, "The soul is freed from the body and after the end of this life, is still suspended in doubt of the coming judgment. And in his book *de bono mortis*, ch. 10, he says: "It was enough to have said to them the souls seek ᾅδην, that is a place which is not seen, which in Latin we call *infernum* [hell]." And in the same place, "The Scripture of Ezra, he calls the dwelling the storage place for souls." And running into human grievances, for the very reason that the just, who preceded, seem even to the day of judgment, through a great period of time, to be defrauded of the reward due to them; he says marvelously that the crowns are similar to the day of judgment; for the day of crowning is awaited by all, that within that day, the conquered will be ashamed and the victors will obtain the palm of victory; therefore, while they await the plenitude of time, the souls await due remuneration; some punishment, others glory.

St. Augustine (lib. 1 *retract.* c. 14) says: "It is rightly asked of those holy men that have already died, whether it can at least be said they are already in possession of it." And in Epistle III *ad Fortunatianus*, explaining certain words of St. Jerome, he says: "In these words there are many things that must be considered of a man of God; first, because according to the very clear teaching of the Lord, even he felt that when we become angels, *i.e.* become equal to the angels, then we are going to see the face of God, which will be, at any rate, in the resurrection of the dead." Likewise in *Enchiridium*, cap. 108, he says: "The time between the death of men and the final resurrection which has been interposed contains souls in hidden receptacles." In book 12 *de Genes.*, cap. 35, he asks what is necessary for souls in the resumption of the body if they can see God without the flesh? He answers: "There can

Ch. I: The Arguments of the Heretics

scarcely be any doubt the mind of man taken from the senses of the flesh and after death itself when the flesh has been laid aside, cannot see such an immutable substance as the holy angels see it." And in book 12 *de civitate Dei*, cap. 9, he says: "The share of a citizen of God will be joined to the immortal angels gathered from mortal men, now mortally tarrying upon the earth, or, in those who have met death, in secret receptacles of souls, and rest in their seats." On Psalm 36, he says: "After this very life you will not yet be where the saints are, in which it will be said: 'Come, ye blessed of my Father, take the kingdom which has been prepared for you from the beginning of the world.' You will not yet be there, and who does not know it? But you can already be in that place where the proud rich man in the midst of his torments saw the ulcerated pauper, resting a long way off. In that rest [of the pauper], you will certainly be secure, awaiting the day of judgment."

St. Bernard, in sermon. 3 on all the Saints, says: "You know, unless I am mistaken, the three states of the souls of the saints: The first clearly in the corruptible body, the second without the body, the third in consummated beatitude; the first in tabernacles, the second in halls, the third in the house of God. ... In that most blessed house of God the souls will enter, not without us, nor without their bodies, *i.e.* the saints not without the people, nor the spirit without the flesh." And in sermon 4, explaining that: *I saw the souls of the slain under the altar*, understands for the altar the humanity of Christ, and says the soul of the martyrs are under the altar because they only see the humanity of Christ; after the day of judgment they will be exalted over the altar to see the essence of God: "Meanwhile they rest happily under the humanity of

Christ, in which, without a doubt, the holy angels long to see from far off, until the time shall come when they are no longer gathered under the altar, but are exalted above it. But when I said, can it be the glory of the humanity of Christ, was it not to speak of men, but the angels who could attain, not to mention conquer? In what way did I say they are going to be exalted over the altar who now rest under it? Indeed in a vision and contemplation, not in display. Let the Son then show to us that he promised himself, not in the form of a slave, but in the form of God; let him also show us the Father and the Holy Spirit, without which nothing would suffice for us in vision."

5) The *fifth* argument is taken from reason: For a judgment and a trial of good and evil men is going to be on the last day; so, the rewards and punishments, are delayed even to that day. Besides, the soul of Christ, after the separation from the body, did not immediately rise up to heaven, but first descended to hell and after the resurrection of the flesh at length ascended into heaven. Therefore, all the saints also after death will be in hell even to the resurrection. For the rest, and resurrection of Christ was the exemplar of our rest, resurrection and ascension; otherwise the disciples and servants would be above their lord and master. To these, the soul and flesh work both good and evil, therefore at the same time, they should not be punished, or rewarded at different times. Lastly, the demons are not yet punished, but spared punishment until after the day of judgment, for on this account they said to Christ: "Have you come here to torture us before the time? And they begged him lest he would command them to go into the abyss." (Matthew 8:29; Luke 8:31). Thus, the same will be done in regard to men: but if the impious are not punished, certainly neither will the pious be rewarded.

Ch. I: The Arguments of the Heretics

Therefore, these are the arguments which are usually asserted against the truth, and we will refute them point by point in the following chapters.

CHAPTER II
We Prove from the Testimony of the Church that the Souls of the Saints Already Enjoy the Vision of God.

NOW, it will be easy to defend the truth from these kinds of arguments. *First*, let the testimony of the Church be added, which says in the prayer in the Divine Office for St. Gregory: "O God, who conferred the rewards of eternal beatitude on the soul of thy servant Gregory, etc." Apart from that prayer, we also have two ecumenical Councils, and the decrees of two Supreme Pontiffs. Accordingly, this very thing was defined in the Council of Florence, in its last session, in the decree of union between the Latins and the Greeks. And in the Council of Trent, sess. 25. Pope Innocent III teaches the same thing in precise words, in *c. Apostolicam*, extra, *de Presbytero non baptizato*. Next, after long disputations, Pope Benedict XII defined it in *Extravaganti*, which begins: *Benedictus Deus*; the whole of which Alonso de Castro relates in *Contra Haereses*, lib. 3, on the word *Beatitudo*.

Furthermore, from that last point we answer the *first* argument of our adversaries. This Benedict XII, who was the immediate successor of John XXII, clearly witnessed that John did not define this question, as he was prevented by death. Now, he not only failed to define it, but he also partly retracted his opinion shortly before his death and partly declared what he did not assert. For he asserted: 1) that in all of his sermons and discourses on the matter, he never intended to define the matter, but only "seek the truth"; 2) He asserted that his earlier opinion displeased him and that he believed the souls of the saints see God even *before* the day of judgment unless the Church and his successors would define it otherwise, to the definition of which he said that he would submit all his opinions. This retraction, made in his own words, is cited by John Villanus in his history (*de rebus Florentinorum*, 11, c. 19), claiming the conversation took place with his brother who abided in the hall of the same Pope John.

Nevertheless, we must list five lies of Calvin from the *Institutes* (IV, c. 7 § 28). The *first* is that Gerson lived in the time of this Pope John, seeing that John died in the year 1334, as all historians witness, and particularly Onuphrius and John Villanus (11, 19). But Gerson was born in the year 1363, as is clear from Trithemius (*de scriptoribus Ecclesiasticis*).

The *second* is that Pope John denied the immortality of the soul. But if this were true, Calvin would deny it so much the more since he pertinaciously defends that souls do not see God. For, Pope John is not accused of any other error by Gerson and others, apart from the error on the vision of God.

Third, that no cardinal opposed himself to Pope John. In reality, as John Villanus writes in his history (*10*, last chapter), a greater part of the Cardinals opposed John and the same is gathered from the decretal of Pope Benedict XII.

The *fourth* is that Philip, the King of France, forbade his own subjects from having communion with Pope John until he would come back to his senses. But as Villanus writes (*loc. cit.*), the king only wrote to the Pope in an amicable and friendly manner to warn him about his opinions because they seemed to sow the seeds of error.

The *fifth* is that the Pope was compelled to recant by the king. But the aforesaid Villanus writes that Pope John only *retracted* his opinion the day before he died at the persuasion of his relations, who feared lest some note of suspicion would be branded on the memory of Pope John

Ch. II: The Testimony of the Church

if the Church would later define the contrary—as it did. See what we wrote on this affair in book 4 of *On the Roman Pontiff*, ch. 14.

CHAPTER III
The Same Is Proven by the Testimony of the Scriptures.

IN the *second* place, we advance the testimonies of the Scriptures. The first is Ecclesiasticus [Sirach] 11:28, "It is easy to reward every man according to his works before God on the day of death."

Someone will say: "Scripture does not say that everyone is rewarded according to their works on the day of their death but that he can be rewarded if God were to choose. But certainly "it is easy" does not mean God can if he wills, but "God rewards and he easily rewards each man according to his works on the day of death." Otherwise, if God could reward according to works but did not, the wise man would have used this argument to rouse us to do good in vain. Besides, when the same Holy Spirit says in verse 29: "in the end of a man is the uncovering of his works," he shows even in the end of a man he is rewarded according to his works. That judgment is made for this purpose, and the uncovering of works that reward would follow.

But one may insist: When these words were written an essential remuneration was not given on the day of death, but only rest in the bosom of Abraham. Consequently, by these words, "It is easy to reward every man on the day of death, etc.," it is merely deduced that on the day of death a certain hope of future beatitude is given to the just, as well as rest in the bosom of Abraham.

I respond: When the text of Sirach says: "reward is given on the day of death," it was understood remuneration is given, "which is able to be held for the diversity of seasons". At that time, heaven was not yet re-opened, while now it has been re-opened by Christ; then the customary rest was given to the just, now true happiness. Hence, in Numbers 35:28, the Lord commands that after the death of the high priest all exiles may return to the country; for this is a figure of our affairs. We are all exiles, our country is paradise, Christ is the high priest, after whose death the entrance to heaven is open to the sons of Adam.

Another testimony, and by far more clear is that of the Apostle Paul in 2 Corinthians 5:1: "For we know, if our earthly house of this habitation were dissolved, that we have a building of God, in a house not made with hands, eternal in heaven. For in this also we groan, desiring to be dressed in our habitation which is in heaven, yet so that we be found clothed, not naked. For we who are also in this tabernacle do groan, being weighed down, seeing that we would not be unclothed, but clothed so that which is mortal may be swallowed up by life."

Note *firstly*, that "if our earthly house," is understood by some authors (as Chrysostom relates) on this sensible world, as if the Apostle were to say, if this world will perish, another better will not be lacking to us after the resurrection. But this is false: for the common opinion of the Greeks and the Latins receives this mortal body for "this earthly house", namely the present, corporal life: and the reason is because at the end of the previous chapter (v. 16) the Apostle says: "If our outward man is corrupted, the inward man is renewed from day to day." Therefore, what he says here about an earthly home is in regard to the outer man. "Besides," he says more clearly below, "while we are in the body, we are away from the Lord." Clearly, in that place he calls the body what he previously called the outward man, the earthly house, the tabernacle, etc.

Note *secondly*, by the eternal and heavenly house, which the Apostle opposes to the earthly house, is understood by the fathers, either as the immoral body

Ch. III: The Testimony of Scripture

(Chrysostom, Theophylactus, Theodoret, Ambrose), or even eternal life, that is the vision of God. And without a doubt, the second exposition is truer, which is of Photius (cited by Oecumenius), Anselm and St. Thomas on this passage of Scripture. In the first place, the Apostle speaks about the present; if this earthly house is dissolved, we have another eternal one in heaven; for he ought to say if he spoke in regard to the glorious body, we will have, not that we have, seeing that we do not yet have an immortal body in heaven.

Besides, the Apostle, when he says if this house is dissolved, he means to say we have another: but if he understands by house the eternal, heavenly body, it is not true that a home will never be lacking for us, since we will not have a body from the day of death even to the day of resurrection. *Additionally*, he calls this very thing the heavenly home, which a little earlier he had called "the eternal weight of heaven" (4:17). After he said: "For that our tribulation which presently is momentary and light, exceedingly and above measure works an eternal weight of glory in us, while we do not look at the things which are seen, but at the things which are not seen. For the things which are seen are temporal; but the things which are not seen are eternal." So in 5:1 he adds, explaining: "For if this our earthly house, etc." Yet, by that: "eternal weight of glory", everyone understands essential beatitude itself.

Unless here the Apostle understood beatitude for "heavenly house", he could not correctly make the conclusion which he does a little further down in verse 6: "Therefore, always taking heart, knowing that while we are in the body, we journey away from the Lord.... But we do take heart, and have a good will rather to be away from the body, and to be present with the Lord." For it doesn't follow that if the mortal body is corrupted we will have another immortal one after the resurrection, therefore, it is good to die now and be away from the body, nay more, the contrary follows, namely it is not good to die even until the day of the resurrection, because even if the immortal body is better than the mortal one, nevertheless, a mortal body is better than nothing. But if through "heavenly house," we were to understand beatitude, the argumentation of the Apostle is the best, namely that: If this mortal life perishes, we have immediately and by far another better one in heaven; therefore, it is good to die faster in this world so that we might live faster in heaven.

Someone will say: It does not seem that beatitude can be called a house, for it has no similitude with a house such as the body has; for the body really is the house of the soul.

I respond: beatitude can be called the best house because it is so great that the soul does not take it and rather the soul enters into it, than it into the soul. Hence in 1 John 3:20, it is said: "God is greater than our heart." And because it is said in John 14:2: "In the house of my Father there are many mansions," everyone understands this to be about different degrees of beatitude. This house is also spoken of in Matthew 25:23: "Enter into the joy of your Lord." And the Apostle elegantly opposes this house to bodily life, or the body itself, for two reasons. 1) He calls the body itself the earthly home because it is made from the earth; he calls the blessed life the heavenly house, because it is found in heaven; for there is the seat of God, and there it always seems like a king in his splendor; 2) He says the body is a house which is dissolved, because it fails daily more and more, but he calls the other eternal because it will always remain in the same state, and at length calls it not made by hand, insinuating that the body which we

Ch. III: The Testimony of Scripture

have was made by hands, namely by the work of humans who begot it, and nourish as well as sustain it with food and drink: but that heavenly house does not depend upon the work of men, but on God alone, manifesting himself to us.

The *third* testimony is a little below in verse 4: "For, we also who are in this tabernacle do groan, being weighed down, since we would not be unclothed, but clothed. ... Therefore, always taking heart, knowing that while we are in the body, we are away from the Lord. For we walk by faith and not by sight. But we do take heart, and have a good will to be away rather from the body, and to be present with the Lord." Note here that the Apostle teaches that there are two desires in us, one of nature to live corporally, the other of grace to see God; and indeed, pious men certainly would fulfill both at the same time if they could, but when they cannot they place the desire of grace ahead of the desire of nature and hence long for the death of the body so that they would be able to live with God. On the other hand, impious men recall everything to the life of the body and the desire of nature.

From the aforesaid we deduce an evident argument on behalf of our teaching: for if we cannot see God until after the resurrection, Paul would not have said that he desires to be away from the body so that he would not be away from the Lord. By these words he shows that there is some state of the soul in which a journey is made from the body and not from the Lord; but such a state would never exist unless we saw God before the resurrection. For in this life we journey from the Lord, but not from the body; in the next life, after the resurrection, we will not journey either away from the Lord or from the body; before the resurrection, however, one necessarily would have to journey from the Lord and from the body. This is why, for the state to be granted in which we travel from the body but not from the Lord, about which Paul is speaking, it is necessary that before the resurrection, when the spirits of the just are freed from the body, they will see the Lord. Nor can it also be said that Paul speaks about a certain imperfect beatitude that consists in the vision of the humanity of Christ where one journeys from the Lord and is made to journey from the presence of the humanity of Christ. Accordingly, the holy Apostle says: "While we are in body we journey from the Lord; we walk by faith and not by sight." It follows from this that the contrary, to not journey from the Lord is not to walk by faith, but to see the species of divine beauty face to face. For the same Apostle, just as he says here, "We walk by faith and not by sight," also says in 1 Corinthians 13:12, "We see now through a looking glass in a confused state, but then we shall see face to face." But a man that sees only the humanity of Christ still has faith and is a pilgrim, and a wayfarer as all writers uphold.

The *fourth* testimony is Luke 23:43: "Today you will be with me in paradise." Here we must note that paradise is received in two ways in the Scriptures: 1) In the mode of a type of garden of corporal delights, in which the first man was constituted before he sinned, about which Moses speaks in the second and third chapters of Genesis; 2) in the mode of the glory of the blessed, of which the first paradise was but a figure. This is what Paul speaks about in 2 Corinthians 12:4, where he says that he was taken up into paradise. For explaining what paradise is, he says he was taken up to the third heaven.

Euthymius, commenting on this passage of Luke, thought (namely to confirm his own error), that here the

Ch. III: The Testimony of Scripture

Lord spoke about an earthly paradise, and consequently writes that the Lord did not answer the thief that *today you will be with me in my kingdom*, but in *paradise*, that he might show the kingdom to be one thing and paradise another. And because someone could object that Christ said "You will be with me in paradise," and still Christ is not in an earthly paradise but a heavenly one, Euthymius answers that Christ is everywhere because he is God, and hence is with the thief and the other saints in an earthly paradise and at the same time with the angels in the heavenly paradise.

It is beyond doubt that this exposition may and must be rejected. 1) The earthly paradise is a place of delights for the body, not soul. For what does it benefit the soul to abound in fruits, herbs, waters and the other earthly things of that paradise? When Christ promised paradise to the thief, he promised a garden of delights *suitable to him*, i.e. spiritual delights.

2) When terms of the New Testament are ambiguous they should preferably be received as they are taken in other passages of the Old Testament; but that term *paradise*, is received in the New Testament for the spiritual paradise, as is clear in 2 Corinthians 12:4 and so in Luke 23:43 they must be received for the spiritual paradise.

3) Christ promised his fellowship when he said: "You will be with me in paradise," and he did not enter an earthly paradise but a heavenly one. Nor does the response of Euthymius avail since in that mode, in which Christ is everywhere, he was also with the thief in this world when he still carried out robbery, and thus Christ would have promised nothing new to him.

Furthermore, Theophylactus, relates and refutes two other expositions of this passage made by others. The *first* is of those who said that heavenly paradise was promised to the thief but it was going to be given after the resurrection, seeing that Christ said "Today you will be," on account of the certitude of a future thing, in the same way that the Prophets often express future things with the present or past tense, such as when the Lord says: "He who does not believe has already been condemned." The *second* is "today" modifies "I say" not "you will be," in this manner: *Amen today I say to you, that you will be with me in paradise.*

But neither of these is solid; not the *first*, both because it is not fitting to make it figurative and leave behind the proper signification of words when otherwise some absurdity would follow, and also because these are not prophetic words which are fitting to be veiled with obscurity, rather, they contain a simple promise and hence must be understood *simpliciter*. And in that passage, "he who does not believe has already been condemned," the past is not received for the future, for the Lord meant to say that he will be judged for certain, but truly he has already judged and condemned himself, seeing that he refused to embrace the faith whereby he could be saved.

The second exposition is clearly ridiculous. What was the Lord talking about when he said: "Amen I say to you today"? Wouldn't the thief see that the Lord spoke about that day? *Besides*, who does not see that the adverb *today* is an answer to the other adverb *when*, which the thief had asked? The thief had said: "Remember me when you come into your kingdom." The Lord responded that *today* will be the *when*, hence *today* you will be with me in my kingdom, and paradise. Thus, the true exposition is of Theophylactus, Ambrose, Bede and others who understand for paradise *the kingdom of heaven*. Christ declared his

Ch. III: The Testimony of Scripture

kingdom is paradise, *i.e.* the highest and eternal happiness lest perhaps the thief would understand something human for "kingdom".

The *fifth* testimony is of Ephesians 4:8, "Christ ascending on high, lead captivity captive." In that passage, by the word "on high", nothing can be understood except the highest heaven. For, even if some understand the cross, just the same Paul explains himself a little later when he says in verse 10: "He that descended is the same also that ascended above the heavens." Hence, by the word "captivity", which he led with himself into heaven, what can be understood but the multitude of the holy souls which he carried out from limbo to heaven, as Ambrose explains?

Now someone will say: "It does not follow that the saints are in heaven, therefore, they see God. I respond: It rightly follows, for by heaven we understand the seat, and as it were, the royal hall of God where God is always seen, for in Isaiah 66:1 it is said: "Heaven is my seat," and in Matthew 5:34 "Do not swear by heaven because it is the throne of God," and Matthew 18:10, "Their angels in heaven always see the face of my father." And in the Lord's prayer we say: "Our Father, who art in heaven." Even if God is everywhere, nevertheless, it is said properly that he is *in heaven* because by the manifestation of himself he shows himself present there, and that is discerned from those who are worthy of that heavenly seat. This is why Cyril elegantly says that heaven is the *veil of the Godhead* (*Catechesi* 9), in which it is clear to us that God is hidden from those of us who are outside the veil. Nay more, Blessed Paul in Hebrews 9:11, compares the entry of Christ into the heavenly sanctuary with the entry of the priest beyond the veil into the Holy of Holies, indicating that it is the same heaven in respect to the divine essence, which was veiled in respect to the ark of the Covenant; and certainly in respect to the souls of the Saints, if they do not see God, it does not seem to relate whether they are in a material heaven, or on earth or in another place.

The *sixth* testimony is from Philippians 1:23, "I desire to be dissolved and to be with Christ." But if the souls are preserved in some place outside of heaven, Paul longed in vain since Christ is in heaven.

The *seventh* testimony is of Hebrews 9:8, "The Holy Spirit showing this that the way into the holies was not yet made manifest whilst the former tabernacle was yet standing." What Primasius, Anselm, Theophylactus, and Oecumenius explain on this passage, that the priests could not enter into the Holy of Holies, nor the people, showed that in the whole time of the Old Testament there was no open path to heaven, and therefore, even the most just descended to hell, because they could not at the same time live in a symbol and be symbolized. But after Christ broke the veil of the tabernacle and the figures ceased, now the way of the saints to the heavenly sanctuary was manifested.

The *eighth* testimony is of Hebrews 12:22-23, "You have not come to a mountain that can be touched, ... but to mount Sion, and to the city of the living God, the heavenly Jerusalem, and to the company of many thousands of angels, and to the Church of the firstborn who are written in the heavens and to God the judge of all, and to the spirits of the just made perfect, etc." Here (as Anselm rightly explains), the Church triumphant is described, and in it they are spoken of like cities, first the angels, then the souls of the firstborn, *i.e.* of those who first believed and

Ch. III: The Testimony of Scripture

already died, such as James the Apostle, Stephen and others, who are said to be written down in heaven because they were enrolled and admitted with the angels in the ranks of the heavenly city, in just the way the *Patres conscripti*[1] were said to be senators of Rome. Unless perhaps one would prefer to say that through the Church of the first born, those enrolled in heaven were understood as the souls of the Patriarchs and Prophets reigning with Christ, whereas by the spirits of the perfect the souls of the Apostles and Martyrs. Nevertheless, the teaching is always the same, now the spirits of holy men are already blessed in that beatitude which previously only the holy angels enjoyed.

The *ninth* testimony is in Acts 7:55, where Stephen, when he was about to die, saw the heavens opened and the glory of God, and Christ standing at the right of the Father. But why did he see this except that he would understand that heaven was open to him and he would immediately be received into that glory? For he clearly understood it when he cried out in verse 58: "O Lord Jesus, receive my spirit."

The *tenth* testimony is from Apocalypse 6:11, where individual white stoles are given to the Martyrs, which signifies the glory of the soul; for the other stole, *i.e.* the glory of the body they will have after the resurrection, as St. Gregory understands in his commentary on the fourth penitential Psalm, as well as Bede, Haymo and Anselm on

---

[1] *Translator's note: This part of the exposition is lost coming out of the Latin. In the Roman Republic, the Patres conscripti literally meant the enrolled fathers, the senators who met the wealth requirements and were enrolled in the order of the senate. So in like manner the saints are enrolled as members of heaven.*

this passage, and also St. Augustine in serm. 4 *On the feast of the Innocents.*

The *eleventh* testimony is from Apocalypse 7:14-15, where it is said on these: "These who are clothed with white stoles, ... stand before the throne of God and serve him day and night in his temple." Thus we hold that they are truly in heaven and see God. For, what does it mean that they stand before the throne of God unless they stand in the sight of God and behold him?

Furthermore, from this we can answer the *second* argument that was given in the first chapter. Against the first passage that was introduced I respond in two ways: 1) Chrysostom in Matthew 20 advises that it is not fitting to square parables in every possible way, but only to consider their *scope*, for many are said not to show something, but only that *the whole story may be seen.* Just the same, the knife is made to cut, still it does not cut from every side; otherwise, in what way do the workers murmur when they receive their farthing? Will they murmur in heaven? And why did the Lord say, "Is your eye evil because I am good?" Will there be an evil eye in heaven? Likewise, how can it be that the wage was first rendered to the last before the first when it is certain that all the elect are going to be given the kingdom of heaven together? Therefore, we only have from that parable of the laborers that the fathers of the New Testament labor for a shorter time than the fathers of the Old Testament did. Nevertheless, they arrive at the same beatitude, or, certainly those who are converted in old age have a shorter labor than those who were in adolescence and yet they can attain no less reward.

2) We can also answer, if we would have it that part of it were to mean in which it is said those who were called in the evening are all the workers, and together all the

Ch. III: The Testimony of Scripture

workers were paid, we will say that through evening is meant the coming general judgment, in which the perfect reward was rendered to all; but still, the judgment does not exclude particular judgments of God in which in death each one is rendered part of the wage individually.

To the second passage from Paul, where he says the fathers did not receive the promises but that they would in their own time, I say three things. 1) By the "promise" the *incarnation of Christ* can be understood, as Primasius explains, for God promised that most often to the fathers Abraham, Isaac, Jacob and David, which is why the Lord says: "Many kings and prophets wished to see what you see, and did not see it."

2) I say that by *promise*, the *beatitude of the soul* may be understood, and then the men of the Old Testament are compared with the men of the New Testament, so that the sense would be: the ancient saints died and did not receive the promise of eternal life, so that they would not surpass us, rather they waited even to the arrival of Christ so that they would receive the promise with us. In other words, they would receive it with the saints of the New Testament. And the Greek text favors this exposition: ο κ ἐκομίσαντο την ἐυαγγελείαν that is, they did not receive the promise, *i.e.* now indeed they received, but still do not yet receive it.

3) I say that through the word "promise" *perfect beatitude of the body and of the soul* is understood, which they still did not have, lest they would have it without us, which is the common exposition of the fathers on that passage. Moreover, we must note the words of Augustine in *tract. 49* of John, "Lest they might be consummated without us." For, he does not say, lest they might be rewarded without us, but lest they might receive the

consummated reward without us, not only of the soul, but also of the body.

To the *third* passage from the epistle of John, I respond: "when he appeared," does not mean when Christ appeared, but when it appeared what we shall be; as is clear from the aforesaid. For he said in verse 2, "It has not yet appeared what we shall be," and then he adds, "for we know that when he appeared," namely what we shall be, "We will be like unto him, because we will see him as he is." Consequently, "we will be like unto him," means we will be like Christ in the sight of the whole world; they will see us in the clouds sitting with Christ and like to him in regard to external glory of the body. Such a glory is borne from the fact that we will see him as he is, for to see God is beatitude of the soul, from which the glory of the body is born. Moreover, this passage is similar (as Bede also advises), to that passage of Paul in Colossians 3:3-4, "You are dead, and your life has been hidden with Christ in God, since Christ appeared, who is your life, then even you will appear with him in his glory." This is why it is not gathered from the words of John that the holy men are not going to see God before the day of Judgment, but only before that day *they are not going to be manifested in glory before the whole world.*

To the fourth passage from the Apocalypse, I say that by "the altar," which the souls are under, cannot be understood some place outside of heaven, seeing that in 7:15 we have those souls clothed with white stoles that are before the throne of God, and serve God day and night in his temple, *i.e.* in heaven.

Thus, there are three Catholic explanations. *The first* is of Bede, that "under the altar," is joined with "of those that were killed," in this way: "I saw the souls of those who

Ch. III: The Testimony of Scripture

were killed under the altar," so for the altar Christ is understood, so that the sense would be, "I saw the souls of those killed under the altar, *i.e.* in witness for the Christian name, just as how in 2 Maccabees 7:36, the Maccabees are said to have been killed under the Covenant of God, that is for the Covenant of God.

The *second* is of the same Bede, as well as Primasius and Haymo which understands "under the altar" to be joined with *I saw*, but for the altar secret understanding is understood, whence proceeds incense of divine praise. For, just as the ark was in the tabernacle, and before the ark a golden altar of incense, so in heaven, in the tabernacle not made by human hands, is the ark of the humanity of Christ wherein divinity resides, and before it is the golden altar whence proceeds perpetual incense of divine praise and prayers. Haymo also notes that, just as in the material tabernacle, between the golden altar and the ark, there was a veil that was broken during the death of Christ, so also, during the Old Testament, the souls of the saints were under the altar, sacrificing holocausts of praise, but the veil was between them and God. Then, after the veil was torn by Christ the altar is now joined to the ark, and there is nothing in between. Moreover, souls are said to be under that altar but not at the altar, to mean that heavenly secret which not only our eyes cannot penetrate, but even our minds. For who could understand how souls will stand before God and minister to him in heaven?

Third is of Anselm who teaches that for the altar Christ is understood. For the sacrifices of the saints, whether of praise or of prayers, do not please God unless they are placed upon this altar, that is they are offered through Christ. Moreover, the souls are said to be under Christ not because Christ is to them a wall overshadowing and impeding them, so that they would see God less as St. Bernard seems to explain; rather, they are said to be under Christ because they are in a lower place both by dignity and because they conquered by the patronage and protection of Christ and they refer the rewards they received to him.

CHAPTER IV
The Same Truth Is Confirmed by the Greek Fathers.

NOW it follows that after the Sacred Scriptures, we also proceed to the testimonies of the Fathers, and first of all the Greek Fathers lest the Greeks of today would think their error could be defended from the testimony of the ancients.

1) Ignatius, in his epistle to the Romans, says that by martyrdom he will embark from this world to God and again he says: "The living water remains in me, inwardly it says to me: 'come to the father'." But according to the error of the Greeks, and the Calvinists, he did not go to God, but to hell or, to another place outside of heaven where God is no more present than here with us. Further, he says in the same place: "Permit me to gaze upon the pure light, so, arriving there I will be a man of God... Now I am miserable, until I will merit to arrive unto God." Why would he not very clearly make it known that by death he was going to be with God right away and to see the pure light of divinity? Thereafter he more often repeats that by martyrdom he is going to come unto Christ. But how will he do so if Christ is in heaven and he will be in hell, hidden away in I know not what receptacles?

2) Dionysius the Areopagate,[1] in his book *de Eccless. hierarch.* (7:1), speaking about the saints constituted in death says: "They know that they will secure a most deserved rest by the species of Christ, when they have come to the goal of this present life. They see more clearly

---

[1] Translator's note: More recent scholarship has shown that Dionysius the Areopagate did not write the works attributed to him. This was not yet in doubt in Bellarmine's time, nor does it weaken the force of his argument since they are still an early witness.

their road to incorruption has already come nearer, extol the gifts of the Godhead, and are filled with a Divine satisfaction, no longer fearing the fall to a worse condition, but knowing well that they will hold firmly and everlastingly the good things which they have already acquired." Note, Dionysius says the souls of the saints attain immortality immediately after death, and since this cannot be understood to be concerning natural immortality, or the immortality of the flesh, it must necessarily be understood about *beatitude*, which is the eternal life of the soul. And in the same book (7:3), he says the souls of the saints are constituted in the region of the living, in the bosom of Abraham, Isaac and Jacob, and adds: "It is evident, then, as I think, that these, the rewards of the pious, are most blessed. For what can be equal to an immortality entirely without grief and luminous with light. Especially if all the promises which pass man's understanding, and which are signified to us by signs adapted to our capacity, fall short, in their description, of their actual truth. For we must remember that the saying is true, that "Eye hath not seen, nor ear heard, neither hath entered into the heart of man to conceive, the things which God has prepared for them that love Him." "Bosoms" of the blessed Patriarchs, and of all the other pious men, are, in my judgment, the most divine and blessed inheritances, which await all godly men, in that consummation which grows not old, and is full of blessedness." But certainly, this does not fit anything but eternal beatitude which alone remains our desire.

3) St. Justin who, in quest. 75 proposed by the gentiles (although, these questions do not seem to be of Justin but of someone more recent), says: "But, after the exit of the soul from the body, right away a distinction is made

Ch. IV: The Testimony of the Greek Fathers

between good and evil men, for they are led to the places which are worthy for them, by the angels, the souls of the good [go] into paradise where the way of life is both the sight of the angels and archangels, and the vision of Christ the savior, from those very words, he departs from the body and is present before the Lord; but the wicked to the places of hell, etc." There note that our opinion is proved not only from what he says, that the souls of the good are led to paradise where the Angels are as well as Christ, but even more from that passage of Paul which Justin posits on his behalf (as we said above). To be present before the Lord means to *see God*, since the opposite is to be away from the Lord and walking by faith.

And also, from this passage it will be easy to respond to those citations brought from Justin to the contrary in the first chapter. For in *quaest.* 60, where he says the tale of Lazarus is not history because reward has not yet been given, he speaks about perfect retribution, when the whole man will rejoice in body and soul, or be tortured. And because in that story mention is made of corporal punishment, it is said: "... that he might cool my tongue because I am tortured in this flame" (Luke 16:24). Therefore, Justin says that the relation is not historical because the condemnation of corporal members has not yet taken place. In question 76, certain gentiles asked if before the resurrection there were no rewards for works, why was the thief brought into paradise? But Justin does not admit the preceding, nay more he shows that for the most part there is remuneration because the soul of the thief is in the body of the blessed and sees the lower places, as well as angels and demons. But he did not call to mind the vision of God because the Greeks do not customarily speak of a vision except of a thing which is *fully* grasped, and therefore he partly denies that a creature can see God, but that the thief saw God *in some manner*, when he says he was in the body of the blessed.

4) St. Irenaeus says (I:10), "To the just and righteous, and to those who keep his commandments, and persevere in his love, some indeed from the beginning, but some from repentance, he that gives life confers by way of a gift incorruption and clothes them with eternal glory." Note, *to some*, that is, those who die right after baptism or who lay down their life for Christ; or finally to the perfect is given immediately life and eternal glory; to others not, except after repentance, that is, satisfaction made in the world to come. For this opinion of Irenaeus is very similar to that of Cyprian (IV:2 *ad Antonianum*): "It is one thing to favor forgiveness and another to attain to glory; it is one thing to be sent into prison not to go out from it until he has paid the last penny, and another to immediately receive the reward of faith and virtue; it is one thing to be corrected after being tried by long suffering for sins and to be purged at length by fire, and still another to be purged of all sins by passion."

Therefore, the same Irenaeus, when he says at the end of book five that the souls of the Saints are led into an invisible place and after the resurrection journey to the Lord with their bodies, he does not mean they are not in heaven in the meantime, or that they do not see God. Rather, he only means they are not now in that *perfect* beatitude where Christ is, who is blessed in soul and body.

And this is confirmed from many conjectures. *Firstly*, because in this passage he says Christ descended to hell to extract and save the souls of the saints. If he extracted them, they are no longer there; and if he saved them, certainly they see God; for this is the salvation of souls.

Ch. IV: The Testimony of the Greek Fathers

Secondly, when he said Christ descended to hell before he rose again and adds the disciples ought to imitate their master, still he does not venture to say the souls of the disciples descended to hell, but says they are led to the invisible place that there they might await the resurrection, and through the invisible place what forbids one from understanding *heaven* where there is an unapproachable light?

Thirdly, because Irenaeus contends that the disciples ought to imitate Christ in [his] death, rest, and the resurrection; but Christ, right after death, was not blessed in body, but rested for three days in the tomb. Still, in the meantime, he was blessed in soul and in paradise. For he said: "Today you will be with me in paradise," consequently, the saints also, while they rest in the tombs in regard to their bodies, are blessed in paradise in their soul.

5) Next is Origen, who takes our part in the very passages that are asserted against us. In *Homily* 7 on Leviticus, he says the saints now have joy, but not perfect, because still their body, *i.e.* that blessed city, is not full, but when we will also be where they are, then they will have perfect joy. And he adds that Christ also does not have perfect joy because he does not yet have all his members. Therefore, he clearly speaks about *accidental* joy. But in *Periarchon* (book 2), in the last chapter, he says a great many of the saints are first led to some earthly place that there they might be despoiled and taught many things which they did not know; thereafter they are led to towering places and there learn some more sublime things, and at length above the heavens to Christ and there see perfectly the causes of all things. In the same book he asserts Paul and the like are perfect there, and see all

things in God. Still, he certainly does err in that he would have it that little by little the saints accomplish things in another life, but he clearly affirms that many of them are now in heaven and see God.

6) St. Athanasius says in his life of St. Anthony that Anthony saw the soul of Ammonis conveyed to heaven surrounded by angels.

7) St. Basil in his homily on the forty martyrs says: "The earth does not conceal you, rather heaven receives you, the gates of paradise are open unto you," and in his oration for the martyr Gordius: "For there was a feeling not that he was to go into the hands of a magistrat but as if he were going to consign himself into the hands of angels. As soon as he was at rest, they came to ferry him, now taken up, to the blessed life."

8) St. Gregory Nazianzen, in his oration on St. Basil, says: "Yet may thou gaze upon us from above, thou divine and sacred person; either stay our thorn in the flesh by your entreaties, given to us by God for our discipline, or prevail upon us to bear it boldly, and guide all our life towards that which is most for our profit. And if we be transported thence, do thou receive us there also in your own tabernacle, that, as we dwell together, and gaze together more clearly and more perfectly upon the holy and blessed Trinity, of which we have now in some degree received the image, our longing may at last be satisfied, by gaining this recompense for all the battles we have fought and the assaults we have endured." And in the oration on Gorgonia, he says that she enjoys the most pure illumination of the Trinity with the angels, she presents her whole self to contemplate with her whole mind.

9) St. Gregory of Nyssa, in his oration on St. Ephraim. "His soul sits in heavenly tabernacles where there are

Ch. IV: The Testimony of the Greek Fathers

ranks of angels, the people of the patriarchs, the choirs of prophets, the seats of the apostles, the joy of martyrs, the joy of the pious, the splendor of the doctors, the renowned body of the firstborn and the pure songs of rejoicing. ... But you, assisting at the divine altar as well as the prince of life, making sacrifice to the most holy Trinity with the angels, remember all of us and beg forgiveness for our sins."

10) St. John Chrysostom, in *Homily* 10 on the first letter to the Corinthians, speaking about beatitude says: "For if the conception of this thing, although a faint sort of one, affords so great pleasure; think how great the gladness, the manifest experience itself shall bring us. Blessed, and thrice blessed, yea, thrice blessed many times, are they who enjoy those good things; just as, consequently, pitiable and thrice wretched are they who endure the opposite of these."

In his third homily on the epistle to the Philippians, he says: "Sinners, wherever they are, are far from the King. Consequently, they are subjects for tears; while the just, be they here, or be they there, are with the King; and there, in a higher and nearer degree, not through an entrance, or by faith, but "face to face'." And in the Greek text, this famous passage is no different: Ὅιδε δίκαιοι, ἂυτε ἐν ταῦθα, ἂντε ἐχεῖ. μετά το βασιλέως εἰσί, κακε μάλλον, καὶ ἐγγύτερον, ὀυδιὰ εἰσόδου, ὀυδιὰ πίσεως, ἀλλά πρόσωπον, πρὸς πρόσωπον. He repeats the same words in homily 69, *ad pop.* and in a homily on the verse of Wisdom 3:1, *The souls of the just are in the hand of God.*

Again, the same Chrysostom, in homily 4 on the epistle to the Philippians, explaining the verse: *What I shall choose I know not*, etc., says: "What do you say, O Paul? When you are about to change from earth to heaven, and to be with

Christ, do you not know what to choose? ... What athlete will desire to fight more when he has already won the crown?" etc. He says the same thing in homily 2 in his epistle to the Romans, that now the soul of Paul lives in the highest heaven near the very throne of the king, where the cherubim and seraphim fly. *On the priesthood*, book 5, he says they who receive the Lord's body purely, in their last hour, surrounded by angels will be lead straight into heaven. From these witnesses, Chrysostom's opinion is clear.

This is why I say to one of the objections raised from Chrysostom in the first chapter (*Hom.* 39 1 Cor.), that he did not mean to say the soul does not enjoy eternal goods before the resurrection, rather, he simply meant that they will not enjoy any heavenly goods *if the flesh does not rise*, since, without a doubt, seeing that both soul and body labored, it is reasonable that each part should have its reward. But if one will not have its reward, from there it is gathered that neither shall the other. And on the other hand, if the flesh will rise in its time and will be crowned, it is gathered that now the soul lives in the presence of God and is crowned. See Theophylactus, for when writing on the same passage of Paul he proposes the sense of Chrysostom more clearly.

I say to the other passage of Chrysostom, which was raised in the first chapter, that he speaks about a crown, or glory *of the body*, on which even Paul speaks. And we answer the same thing in the places objected to the contrary from Theodoret, Theophylactus, and Oecumenius on this passage; for they, as students of Chrysostom himself imitated his commentary.

11) Cyril, the bishop of Jerusalem, speaking about the thief (*Catech.* 13) says: "You will be lead from the wood

Ch. IV: The Testimony of the Greek Fathers

into paradise." And lest we might think he speaks about a place of rest in the bosom of Abraham, he adds: "Faithful Abraham has not yet entered, and the thief enters," etc. And lest we might think he speaks about an earthly paradise, he adds: "Do not fear the serpent, for he fell from heaven and will not cast you out." Therefore, Cyril clearly asserted that the thief was the first of all to enter paradise.

12) Cyril of Alexandria (*in Joann.* lib. 11 cap. 36) says that the souls of the saints do not live on earth after the death of the body, nor are lead to the punishments of hell, but escape into the hands of God the Father, and lest we might think he understood the bosom of Abraham from this, or some place outside of heaven, he says that this journey was first opened and prepared by Christ, so, the souls of the saints do not descend to the place where they went before the death of Christ, and he adds that the souls of the Saints have perpetual life with Christ.

13) Then there is Epiphanius (*Panarion*, heres. 78), who says towards the end: "The saints are in honor, their rest in glory, their departure into perfection, their lot in beatitude, in holy mansions, their omen with the Angels, their rooms in heaven, glory in incomparable honor, and perpetual reward in Christ Jesus our Lord."

14) Theodoret, in *ad Graecos*, book 8, which is on Martyrs, says: "If heaven is the seat of those who lived piously, their departure from this place is the end of their journey, and martyrs have already obtained it; for nobody can be more pious than they, and they bear, far and wide, the fullest honors of all mortals, and are distinguished with eternal crowns." Thus, if they are in heaven and are distinguished with eternal crowns, how would they not obtain the promise (as the same Theodoret says, whom our

adversaries object to us), even if he is talking about the promise of the resurrection and bodily glory?

15) Eusebius (*Hist.* lib. 4 cap. 15) says that Polycarp, through death, has already obtained the rewards of immortality; but what is that immortality, which is given to the soul in place of the reward, immortal by nature, except beatitude? Likewise, in lib. 6, cap. 5, he says of Poramiena: "In this way, that blessed virgin passed from hearth to heaven." You read similar things throughout his work.

16) John Damascene, in his history of Barlaam and Josaphat, near the end: "before the countenance of the Lord, shining and naked, he is presented already before he shall be adorned with the promised crown."

17) Theophylactus, in chapter 23 of Luke, says: "We must say that paradise and the kingdom of heaven are the same; for the thief is in paradise, and in the kingdom, no other place enjoys the perfect participation in goods," etc. There, he amply confutes the opinions of those who would have it that the thief was led to paradise, but not to the kingdom of heaven. So when Theophylactus says in chapter 16 of Luke that the story of the rich man and Lazarus is a parable because the division of rewards and punishments has not yet been made, he speaks about the rewards and punishments *which pertain to the body*, and so he rightly calls the sermon parabolic since it is about the eyes and the tongue of the rich man in hell. When he also says on 11:39 of Hebrews that the saints receive nothing of the heavenly promises, he means to say, nothing of that glory and of those qualities which the resurrection confers upon the body.

18) Oecumenius, in cap. 9 *ad Hebraeos* says that Christ not only entered heaven, but even lead the human race

Ch. IV: The Testimony of the Greek Fathers

with him, that is the many holy fathers who, without a doubt, if they are in heaven with Christ, are also blessed there with him. Otherwise (as we said above) the habitation of corporal heavens would hardly benefit their spirits.

Therefore, we have all the Greek doctors on our side; for only Arethas and Euthymius remain from those who are brought to us in objection. Now, from those citation of Arethas, when he says the saints hope for future glory, this can suitably be understood on the glory *of the body*; moreover, Euthymius cannot be explained, but in this matter it is not even to be greatly marveled at; for he is the most recent of all. He wrote around the year 1180, and in that time the Greeks manifestly began to be heretics and schismatics.

As a confirmation of this point, which we have been advancing from the Greeks, who deny that a creature can see God, St. Augustine responds that those authors, when they say God cannot be seen, speak about *corporal* vision. For, he so explains the words of St. Jerome in epistle 111; for he says Jerome meant to say that the angels do not see God with corporeal eyes, but merely see him *in mind.*

But this answer does not satisfy, for three reasons. *Firstly,* because Jerome and Chrysostom, Theodoret and other authors cited with him assert that angels are spirits, and do not have fiery bodies nor are united to fire, as St. Augustine opined; and at length they deny God is seen by angels.

Secondly, because Jerome, explaining the reason why the angels cannot see God, says that a creature cannot catch sight of its creator; and Chrysostom usually gives the same reasoning. But this reason holds not only for the eyes of the body, but also for eyes of the mind, for both are created eyes.

Thirdly, because these fathers say that God is visible neither to angels nor to men, but only to God himself. But God does not see himself with corporeal eyes, rather with mind. Therefore, these fathers are speaking *about the mind*, not corporeal eyes.

This is why the true answer is from St. Thomas (I q. 12 art. 1) that these fathers understand by the term "vision" *perfect comprehension*, because what we see with the eyes of the body, we perfectly understand. Moreover, what we grasp in this world, we do not understand so perfectly; for we do not have the proper species of substances and especially of separate ones; therefore the language of seeing is not usually taken up for each cognition, but only for that *most perfect*, whereby a thing is grasped. In that genus of vision no one can see God, except *God*. Besides, the error of the Anomeans, saying that God can be grasped by a creature also flourished at that time. Consequently, the Fathers shuddered from the terminology *of seeing*, since they were speaking about the contemplation of God, lest they would seem to admit comprehension.

Someone will say: But Chrysostom says that God was invisible to the angels only to the incarnation of Christ, therefore, he does not speak about comprehension; otherwise it would follow that after the incarnation God could be fully grasped. *I respond:* God, before the incarnation, only existed as God, and therefore was simply incomprehensible; but after the incarnation he became man, insofar as *man* is comprehensible, and this is what Chrysostom meant.

Someone will say *secondly*: Theodoret, (*loc. cit.*) claims the angels do not see God any differently than Abraham,

Ch. IV: The Testimony of the Greek Fathers

Moses and Isaiah and the rest, but these not only did not comprehend him, but did not truly see God in himself, but only in a body taken up by angels, which related God, or by an imaginary revelation.

I respond: Theodoret does not say "no differently", but only to constitute a similitude between the vision of the angels and the patriarchs. And it consists in this, that just as one is imperfect, and not comprehensive, so also the other, although with a great distinction.

CHAPTER V
The same is proven from the testimonies of the Latin Fathers

NOW we add the consensus of the Latin Fathers, so that this faith would be understood to be the faith of the whole Church.

1) Cyprian, in his book on the victory of the Martyrs, last chapter, says: "Who, then, does not with all his powers labor to attain to such a glory that he may become the friend of God, that he may at once rejoice with Christ, that after earthly tortures and punishments he may receive divine rewards? ... In persecutions, the earth is shut up, but heaven is opened; Antichrist is threatening, but Christ is protecting; death is brought in, but immortality follows; the world is taken away from him that is slain, but paradise is set forth to him restored; the life of time is extinguished, but the life of eternity is realized. What a dignity it is, and what a security, to go gladly hence, to depart gloriously in the midst of afflictions and tribulations; in a moment to close the eyes with which men and the world are looked upon, and at once to open them to look upon God and Christ! Of such a blessed departure how great is the swiftness! You shall be suddenly taken away from earth, to be placed in the heavenly kingdoms." He says similar things in his sermon *on mortality*, epist. 2, lib. 4 and more often in other places.

2) Hilary, *in Psalm 64*, says: "Indeed the blessed are those who have already been chosen by God to dwell in his tabernacles; but it is fitting for us to hasten into the consort of this beatitude, awaiting it in work and prayer." And a little before that, those tabernacles were heavenly mansions, which Christ said were in the house of his father. And in Psalm 124, speaking about the Apostles, and

other saints, he says: "How can we not understand the mountains to mean those who now exult, glorious over earthly nature in the things of God?" Therefore, when the same Hilary, in Psalm 138, says the law is of human necessity, that souls descend to hell, it is understood for that time, *in which heaven was closed*; for afterward, Christ ascending into heaven, opened up the entrance to heaven, so that it is no longer necessary to descend to hell.

3) Ambrose (lib. 7 epist. 59 *ad Thessal.*) says: "Ascolius, a dweller of higher places, is an inhabitant of the eternal city, of that Jerusalem which is in heaven, he saw in that place the immense measure of that city, pure gold, a precious stone, perpetual light without the sun and all these things were verified long ago, but now, face to face." See also lib. 10, epist. ult. and in cap. 1, epistl. *ad Philipp.* But why does Ambrose say (*de Cain*, II, 2), that souls are still wavering, in an uncertainty of suspended judgment, and await the examination of time? He means to say the blessed souls do not know when the judgment will be. But in his book on the *Good of Death* (cap. 10), he speaks about the reward of the wage, which must be given both to the soul and the body *publicly* in the sight of the whole world. For that is properly said to be the crown which is publicly given to the victors, and with renown, but here it does not follow that part of the reward is not given before through the particular judgment. Nor is it opposed that Ambrose seems to say all souls descend to hell, for he does not say this, but only proves that the old philosophers said this, because in that time it was true.

4) Prudentius, who sang in his song of St. Agnes:

> O happy virgin, O new glory,
> Noble inhabitant of the heavenly citadel.

Ch. V: The Testimonies of the Latin Fathers

Furthermore, Prudentius repeats other things of this sort in many places. This is why, when he says elsewhere that the souls of the blessed are led to the bosom of Abraham, or to paradise, whence Adam was cast out, he speaks *figuratively*, because both the bosom of Abraham and earthly paradise, are types of the kingdom of heaven, and it is clear from the last passage of Prudentius, for he says the souls are in the bosom of Abraham and at the same time in paradise, since, at length, he constitutes places that were different according to their property; but they are not different according to their meaning.

5) St. Paulinus, who says (*natali 3 de s. Felice*):

> Born in body from the earth.
> Slain, and born for Christ in the stars above.
> A martyr having obtained heavenly honor without blood.

Likewise:

> The glory of heaven surrounds him with a halo of its light;
> blossoming with both the double crown victory, and peace.

6) St. Jerome, in his epistle to Marcella on the death of Lea, says: "For her short labor, she already enjoys eternal blessedness. She is welcomed by choirs of angels, she follows Christ and says whatever we heard, we see in the city of the Lord of hosts." He has similar things in his *epitaph* of Nepotian, Paula, Blaesilia and others.

7) St. Augustine, (*Genesis*, 12, 34) says first that the souls of the saints are in paradise, or in the third heaven,

to which St. Paul was taken up: "Either in the third heaven, or else somewhere else to which the Apostle was taken after the third heaven: still, unless it has been called another thing by different names, there are the souls of the blessed." Next, explaining what this third heaven is, he says: "The third heaven is that which is grasped by the mind so secretly and remotely, and altogether without the senses of the flesh and worldly things. It ineffably avails to see and hear those things which are in that heaven, both the very substance of God, and God the Word, through which all things were made in the love of the Holy Spirit." The same Augustine says in book 20 of *de Civitate Dei*, ch. 13: "But assuredly the victorious souls of the glorious martyrs having overcome and finished all griefs and toils, and having laid down their mortal members, have reigned and do reign with Christ till the thousand years are finished, that they may afterwards reign with Him when they have received their immortal bodies." He says the same in Psalm 119, on that verse: *Woe is me, that my sojourning is prolonged!* "There, all the just and the saints enjoy the word of God without reading or letters, where for us the it has been written by means of a page, but for them they see by the face of God." The same in his book on Meditations, cap. 22: "Happy that soul which, loosed from the earthly body is free to seek heaven, secure and at peace, for it fears no enemy nor death; it has the present, and sees the most beautiful Lord without end, whom it served, whom it loved, and to whom it has at length come unto glorious and rejoicing." And in chapter 24 of the same book: "By this very fact I ask you, who chose you? Who made you such as you are, from whose beauty you are now satiated, from whose immortality you have become immortal, from whose most blessed vision you will always

Ch. V: The Testimonies of the Latin Fathers

rejoice?" Later, St. Augustine, in epistle 111, regards Paul to have seen the essence of God when he was taken up to the third heaven, therefore, how much more must it be believed, that he thought this about the souls of the blessed?

Now we must note two things for the explanation of contrary passages. The first is that Augustine doubted at one time not whether souls had the very vision of God as well as beatitude, but *about the place* where the souls of the blessed reside, and nevertheless he later asserted, after he had diligently considered the matter, the very thing we assert. For on Psalm 36 [37], he says the souls before the day of judgment are not in the kingdom of heaven, but in the bosom of Abraham, as if these places were distinct. In *Confessions*, book 9, ch. 3, he shows that he was uncertain when he says: "Now Nibridius lives in Abraham's bosom. Whatever that may be which is signified by that bosom, there lives my Nebridius, my sweet friend, your son, O Lord, adopted of a freedman; there he lives. For what other place could there be for such a soul? There lives he, concerning which he used to ask me much — me, an inexperienced, feeble one. Now he puts not his ear unto my mouth, but his spiritual mouth unto your fountain, and drinks as much as he is able, wisdom according to his desire —happy without end." Take note that here he asserts the vision and enjoyment [of God], but he is uncertain about the place.

But in book 2 of *Questions of the Evangelists*, ch. 38, (books that he wrote later, as we gather from book 2 of *Retractions*) he so speaks: "The bosom of Abraham is rest of the blessed poor, whose is the kingdom of heaven, in which they are received after this life. ... Abraham's bosom is understood to be the hiding place of the Father, whither after his Passion and resurrection our Lord was taken up, whither He was said to be carried by the angels, as it seems to me, because that reception whereby Christ reached the Father's secret place, the angels announced to the disciples. The rest may be taken according to the former explanation, because that is well understood to be the Father's secret place, where even before the resurrection the souls of the righteous live with God."

Again, in *City of God*, book 20, ch. 15, he clearly says the blessed are not in hell, where Lazarus was previously. So then, he corrected what he had said on Psalm 36, for in that passage of *City of God* he says: "For if it does not seem absurd to believe that the ancient saints who believed in Christ and his then future coming, were kept in places far removed indeed from the torments of the wicked, but yet in hell, until Christ's blood and his descent into these places delivered them, certainly good Christians, redeemed by that precious price already paid, are quite unacquainted with hell while they wait for their restoration to the body, and the reception of their reward."

It is also deduced from this that the secret or hidden receptacles cited by Augustine are not the limbo of the Fathers in hell, but the *hidden place of the Father in heaven*. So three citations are left to be explained, *Enchiridion*, ch. 10, *City of God*, 12, 9, and *on Psalm 36*.

Secondly we must note that Augustine regarded that the souls of the saints indeed see God, but not as perfectly as they will after the resurrection. This is why the natural desire of souls to take up their body again does not prevent them from being born to God with their whole energy, and this is a difference between the angels and men. Angels, since they await nothing more, are wholly borne to God, while the souls of the saints, look partly to God and partly

Ch. V: The Testimonies of the Latin Fathers

to the body. That is clear from what Augustine says *on Genesis* (12, 35), where he first posits the question: Why is the resumption of the flesh necessary for the soul in beatitude? He answers, because the soul cannot see God as the angels do without the flesh. And he explains that this is because there is a certain natural appetite in it to operate the body; so in a certain measure, it is delayed by that appetite from continuing to that supreme good with its full purpose as long as it is not a basis for the body, in whose administration that appetite has repose. So Augustine does not say the soul, when separated from its body, cannot see an incommutable substance, but cannot see it *in that mode*, *i.e.*, as perfectly as the angels see it, on account of the aforesaid cause. For equal reasoning, in *Retractions*, book 1 ch. 14, where he says it is rightly asked whether the souls of the saints are still in possession of beatitude in which the angels are, he explains himself a little earlier, when he says: "But, whether to contemplate the truth of the heart with their eyes, just as it was said, face to face, they have nothing less from this (because clearly they lack their body, which they naturally desire), this is not the place to inquire by disputation, etc." Therefore, he does not doubt whether the souls of the just are in that possession, but *whether they are in such a way that they lack nothing*.

In the same mode we must respond to that passage from epistle 111 to Fortunatianus. There he speaks on *the most perfect* vision, which we do not have until we will become equal with the angels, that will be in the resurrection of the dead. For, now the saints are not equal to the angels, seeing that the angels wholly live and are immortal, but the saints are partly living and partly dead.

Moreover, we must note here that on account of these passages of St. Augustine, the scholastics ask whether the glory of the soul is greater after the resurrection than before? They all agree on two points. 1) The accidental joy of the soul will be greater both extensively, because it will be in soul and in body; and intensively, because the soul itself will rejoice more when it will see its body glorious than now, when it sees it lying dead. 2) The essential joy will be more extensive because now it is in the soul alone, later it will overflow into the body, and will effect that body by its glorious mode.

But they do not agree on the increase of essential glory intensively, for St. Peter Lombard (in 4 *Sent.* dist. 49) and St. Thomas (on the same place, q. 1, art. 4) along with St. Bonaventure (*ibid.*, art. 1, q. 1), Richardus (*ibid.*, art. 2 q. 7) and Marsilius of Padua (*ibid.*, q. 13 art. 3) all say the essential glory will then be greater even intensively, and they understand Augustine to be speaking of this increase.

There are two reasons for this. 1) Because the soul has being more perfectly in the body than outside of it, consequently, it operates more perfectly. 2) Because the soul when separated on account of inclination to the body is distracted and impeded from being borne with its whole intention to God. So due to this remote impediment it operates more intensively. Yet, St. Thomas (1. 2. q. 4 art. 5), Cajetan (*ibid.*) and Durandus (*in 4* dist. 49 q. 7) say on the contrary that the essential glory does not become greater intensively, but only extensively, and on this extensive increase they explain Augustine. Their reasoning is, that if glory increased intensively, or it would happen by reason of the object, whether of light or habit of glory, or potency, it is not by reason of the object, or habit, because these do not increase unless grace increases. Moreover, grace does not increase on the day of judgment because there is no place for new merit after this life; not also on the side of

Ch. V: The Testimonies of the Latin Fathers

potency, because when the soul, in seeing God, does not depend upon a phantasm, it does not depend in any mode on the body, and hence, that operation of seeing God cannot be as perfect in a separated soul as in the soul joined to the body.

Furthermore, I add two things. *Firstly*, the prior opinion is more to the mind of Augustine, and not of Haymo, commenting on chapter 6 of the Apocalypse, as well as Bernard, on whom we will speak of below. For Augustine clearly says something is lacking to a disembodied soul to see God perfectly while it lacks the body. I say secondly, that the second opinion is simply more true, and for this reason St. Thomas rightly changed his opinion. This is why in regard to the first, I say for the first opinion, the soul does not have an better being in the body than outside of it, except *extensively*, because it communicates itself to the body; for otherwise in itself, the existence of the soul is always the same; it does not receive more or less.

I say to the *second*, the inclination toward the body does not impede vision or the love of God by any mode, because it is ordered to the love of God as to an end, just as the love of medicine does not impede a love of health; otherwise the angels, when they are sent to outward matters and compelled to think about them, would be distracted from the vision of God, and the soul itself, when it ought to be occupied in the administration of the body, will be even more distracted than now in desiring the body. Add, that this seems to have been defined by Benedict XII, for in *extravaganti, Benedictus Deus*, he says the vision of God continues which souls have from the death of the body even to the resurrection, and thence, even for eternity; where it seems he says that it neither increases nor diminishes. Moreover, John Villanus (*hist.* 11,

19) says that Benedict defined that the glory of souls does not increase after the resurrection except extensively, so he witnesses that he heard from theologians who were present when it was defined by that Pope. Thus for Augustine.

8) The eighth Latin Father is Prosper of Aquitaine. In his *De vita contemplativa* (1, 1),[1] he says: "Now, according to the saying of Sacred Scripture, *all human life is a temptation upon the earth*, then will the trial end when the fight also ends; then will the fight end when after this life certain victory follows the fight, so that all soldiers of Christ who, to the end of their present life, aided from on high, untiringly resisting their enemies may, when their wearisome journey in foreign parts has at last ended, shall reign happy in their homeland. There, human nature will be so restored and so healed of every single infirmity that no sin will remain in it, nor will it any longer be able to sin. All this will be its reward. Once it has been made partaker of the contemplative life, it will behold without satiety the author of its happiness, rejoice in him, obtain from him that for which it has hoped, and remain forever in the state it has attained by holy living."

9) Maximus of Turin, in his *homily* on Eusebius of Vercelli, says: "Worthily does one reflect on the memory of men who have passed to the joy of the angels." And in his homily on St. Agnes, "He renders unto us forgiveness of sins, who provided the palm of all your labors to you."

---

[1] Translator's note: In Bellarmine's time, this work was ascribed to Prosper of Aquitaine. Today, it is universally conceded to have been written by Julianus Pomerius. This would put it around the close of the fifth century and near the sixth, which would not defeat Bellarmine's purpose in citing it, irrespective of the author.

Ch. V: The Testimonies of the Latin Fathers

10) Pope St. Leo I, who says (*serm. de Sancto Laurentio*): "Cruel savage! You gain nothing, and accomplish nothing. That which can die passes by degrees beyond the reach of your tortures, and when Lawrence departed to heaven, you and your fires were conquered."

11) St. Fulgentius (serm. de S. Stephano) says: "Today, going out from the tent of the body as a soldier, as a triumphant soldier he passed to heaven, that man is going to reign forever as he has ascended to heaven." Likewise: "Today, Stephan was clothed with the stole of immortality."

12) Primasius (cap. 9 *Hebr.*) says: "The heavenly kingdom was inaccessible to mortals, until Christ came, who will open the door of his heavenly kingdom to us after the completion of his passion and uncovering the veil, that is, heaven."

13) Pope St. Gregory on Psalm 4, says: "Beatitude is also attributed to the souls of the saints before the resurrection, and just the same, it will be conferred upon their bodies after the judgment." And in the *Dialogue* (4, 25), he avowedly proves it.

14) Bede, commenting on the *Apocalypse*, ch. 6, says: "The souls of the saints that rejoice in their blessed immortality, have now each one robe. But when their bodies arise, as Isaiah says, 'they will possess double in their own land'."

15) Haymo, speaking on the same passage, says: "First, the robe is the price of Baptism, the reward of martyrdom, the reward of eternity, the joy of heavenly beatitude, etc."

16) Anselm, commenting on 2 Corinthians 5, says: "Preachers of the Church, after they depart from their bodies by no means suffer a period of tarrying, as the ancient fathers were delayed from gaining their heavenly

country. Rather, as soon as they depart from the bond of the flesh they take their refreshment in their heavenly seat."

17) St. Sulpitius, in his epistle to the Deacon Aurelius on the death of Blessed Martin, says: "Although I know that man must not be mourned for, to whom the crown of justice was finally rendered when he conquered and triumphed over the world."

18) St. Bernard, in his epistle to the brethren from Ireland, which is found after his sermons on the feast of All Saints,[1] and the sermon on St. Malachy, says: "God forbid that now, O holy soul (he addresses the dead Malachi) to suppose your prayer less efficacious now, when in his full presence, you supplicate the divine Majesty; nor do you, at this moment, walk in faith but rather reign in glory. God forbid that we consider your abounding charity diminished, much less unemployed for us, when you prostrate yourself before the very foundation of Divine charity, drawing abundantly its copious draughts, when formerly you thirsted for its smallest drops." What could be clearer? He says Malachy does not walk by faith, but faith is not removed except by the vision of the Trinity. He thus says that he enjoys the font of charity, *i.e.* God, in the way that a man that lies down in a fountain enjoys the waters when he draws abundantly with his mouth. He says the same thing in a sermon on St. Malachy, which is found at the end of his life of St. Malachy: "He enjoys equal glory and happiness with the angels." And yet the "Angels always see the face of the Father, who is in heaven" (Matthew 18:10).

---

[1] Translator's note: In the 1835 Benedictine edition of St. Bernard's letters, subsequent to Bellarmine's time, it is listed as the 374th letter.

Ch. V: The Testimonies of the Latin Fathers

We gather the same in epistle 266 to the Abbot Sugerius, which had to do with the soul, where he asks: "What need have you of earthly spoils when you are about to go to heaven to be clothed with the robe of glory? ... That peace awaits you, which surpasses every sense; the just await you, until you partake of your reward; the joy of your Lord awaits you." Now the same man in his fourth sermon on the feast of all saints says that peace, which surpasses all sense, consists in the vision of God, as it is in itself.

Thereafter, in a sermon on the death of Humbert, he says: "Behold, he is in your presence, O most sweet father (Humbert), that fountain of purity, whom you thirsted for with such strength of mind; behold you are immersed in that abyss of divine goodness, whose memory of sweet abundance you customarily announced with such devotion." Likewise, in his fifth sermon on the feast of all saints, treating on the verse: *Be converted unto me in fasting, weeping and mourning* (Joel 2:12), he asks why God is found more in fasting and weeping than in joy and exultation, and he answers by asking: "Why is it that the just man will find him in joy and exultation; but the man that is not yet just, will not except in fasting and prayer? So plainly, rather the just man, who now merits the sight, no longer lives by faith, etc." There he admits that some saints no longer live by faith, but enjoy the sight of God. See also what he writes in his second sermon on St. Victor.

Now, I say to passages on the contrary, that Bernard was a disciple of St. Augustine, and when he says the saints are going to see God by the resurrection, and not before, he does not speak of the simple vision, but on that perfect vision which the soul will have when it is borne to God with its whole force. And this is clear from the third sermon on the feast of All Saints. For he had just said that the holy souls in this life are in tents, after this life even to the resurrection they will be in the hall, after the resurrection they will be in the house of God, *i.e.* in beatitude. He continues, explaining: "Now they received individual robes, but will not be clothed in a two-fold robe until we are also clothed. For the first robe is the very happiness and rest of souls, while the second is immortality and the glory of their bodies, etc."

You see here in the resurrection nothing is added to souls *per se*, except the glory of the body and hence the glory of the soul, which is the vision of God, is given before the resurrection. Moreover, I said *per se* because according to Bernard, the glory of the soul is added, but not per se. Consequently, the vision is more perfect from that because the soul, desiring nothing more, will be borne before God whole, the very thing Bernard explains in the following words: "The souls of the saints which God marked with his own image desire you [O flesh]; their joy is complete without you, glory is perfected, but beatitude cannot be complete. So accordingly, this natural craving is so strong in them that even their whole love and desire does not yet freely go forth towards God; but, as it were, it is indented and wrinkled, since it is inclined to you by desire." Add to these what St. Thomas says in his work *Against the Greeks*, and the Schoolmen commenting at the end of 4. *Sent.* distinction 49.

Therefore, we have the opinion of the Church was that of all the Latin Fathers, with the exception of Tertullian, Lactantius, and Victorinus. Of these, Tertullian was a heresiarch, and Lactantius lapsed into many errors (especially in regard to the coming age, seeing that he was more of an expert in the books of Cicero than of Sacred

Ch. V: The Testimonies of the Latin Fathers

Scripture). As far as the Victorinus, he was indeed a martyr, but, as St. Jerome witnesses in his *Epistle to Magnus*, he was lacking in erudition, although he did not lack the will for erudition.

CHAPTER VI
The Same Is Proven from Arguments that, Although Taken from Reason Nevertheless, Have Their Foundation in the Scriptures.

LASTLY, we add arguments sought from reason itself.

1) The *first* argument can be taken from the punishments of the damned. Supposing God is not more prone to punish than to reward, seeing that the impious are already in torment, it certainly seems just that the righteous gain their rewards. Furthermore, the impious are now in torments, as the Gospel witnesses, for in Luke 16:23 we read: "When the rich man was in torments," etc. Now the Greeks respond that this is a parable, and contains an account of things to come; future things are told as if they were happening in the present for greater efficacy.

On the other hand, *a)* It does not seem to be a parable, but rather a history, not only because in it the proper names of Lazarus, and Abraham are placed and also, the Church venerates that Lazarus as a truly holy man; but also because Ambrose (on Luke 16), Jerome (*in Jovinianum*, lib. 2) and Augustine (*de cura pro mortuis*, cap. 14) as well as Gregory (*Dialogue* 4, 29) all call it a history.

b) Even if it were a parable, it cannot mean future events after the day of judgment, but a matter that is *past*, or *present*. In verse 27, the rich man says, "I ask you father Abraham to send Lazarus to the house of my father." And in verse 29 Abraham answers: "They have Moses and the Prophets, let them hear them." But after the day of judgment men will not be in this world, nor can they hear Moses, and the Prophets. So if the tale were a parable, nevertheless, it shows that now souls are in torment, otherwise it would not be true nor have the appearance of truth.

2) The *second* argument: The whole Church invokes the saints after the coming of Christ. Both the Greek and the Latin Fathers teach the saints must be invoked, yet, before the coming of Christ we do not read that this was customarily done. But if the saints were now also under the earth in the bosom of Abraham, there would be no difference between their state and the state of the saints of the Old Testament.

3) The *third* argument. St. Basil notes at the beginning of his prayer to St. Barlaam: Before the coming of Christ the death of the saints brought tears, whereas after the coming of Christ we celebrate the day of death of the saints with supreme joy. Why would this be, except that then death was a misery, but now it is the beginning of happiness? And it is confirmed, for now we call the day of death a birthday, because clearly the saints dying on earth are born in heaven.

4) The *fourth* argument is from the visions of those who saw some souls in the torments of hell, others in purgatory, and others in paradise. See St. Gregory the Great, (*Dialogue*, 4, 37), as well as St. Bede (*Hist.* 5, 13).

5) The *fifth* argument: At this time the saints have the merit of eternal life. If they do not, then they will never have it, because after the end of life there is no place for new merits and no impediment whereby they can have less than eternal life, seeing that before heaven was closed and now it is open. Therefore, it must be affirmed that now they have received their reward.

6) The *sixth* argument. In Leviticus 19:13, God commanded it to be written: "The wages of him that you have hired shall not abide with you until the morning." Therefore, lest God would seem to oppose himself, he will

Ch. VI: Arguments from Reason

not retain the reward of the saints even to the consummation of the world.

7) The *seventh* argument. In Proverbs 13:12, we read: "Hope that is deferred afflicts the soul," but it is not fitting that they are afflicted who have no sin.

From these the opposing arguments in chapter 1 are answered. *Ad primum*, I say: the day of general judgment belongs to the future, and then it will be rendered to each man according to his works; still, another *particular* judgment precedes that judgment, in which it is also rendered to each man according to his works. Now, these are not opposed to one another, as in the first judgment the rewards are rendered *privately*, while in the later *publicly* and *manifestly*. Just the same, the day of general judgment is called the day of the Lord, not because other days are not of the Lord, but because it will manifestly be the day of the Lord, and so manifestly that no man, be he Epicurus or Atheus, will not at that time confess that it is the day of the Lord. This is in the same manner as among merchants, where a certain day is called the day of payment, not because payments are not due on other days, but because that day has been constituted for this very purpose, so that payments shall be made; so also, a certain day is called the day of judgment and retribution, not because God does not judge on other days, but because that day was constituted for this purpose, that judgment and retribution should take place.

Now, someone will say: Does it not seem vain that there will be a future judgment if the rewards are already given? What is rendered, whether it has been rendered openly or secretly?

I respond: It will not be in vain. There are five reasons on account of which there will be a general judgment, even if a particular judgment precedes it. 1) The *first is*, that the justice of God as well as his mercy will be shown. God made all things to show his glory, but now he does not so clearly do so, and men are found that would accuse God of injustice or that do not believe in his providence because they see good men are afflicted and evil men rejoice. Thus, God chose for himself one day where he will show his justice before the whole world against the impious and his supreme mercy to the pious, while at the same time, he will show himself with supreme mercy towards the just, but no cruelty or injustice against the impious; and with supreme severity towards the impious, but no respect of persons or unjust liberality toward the pious.

2) The *second* reason is that the Son of man would be glorified, as it pertains to the glory of Christ. In his first coming he was unjustly judged as a guilty man, and will appear again glorious and a judge and it will fulfill that of Isaiah 45:24, "I live that every knee shall be bowed to me;"[1] which Paul explains in Romans 14:11 is about Christ's future judgment.

3) The *third* reason is for the praise of the good, but ignominy for the wicked. God willed that the saints, as they became a spectacle in their struggles in the world before angels and men, will also be pronounced victors before angels and men. Thus Paul, wherever he speaks about the judgment, usually advances this reason as he does in Romans 2:16, 1 Corinthians 4:9, and other places.

---

[1] Translator's note: The vulgate that Bellarmine used has *Vivo ego, quia mihi curvabitur omne genu*, whereas the subsequent revision under Pope Clement VIII omits *vivo ego*.

Ch. VI: Arguments from Reason

4) The *fourth* reason is that the whole man will be judged and receive his reward. For now only souls are judged and they receive part of the reward.

5) The *fifth* is that the good and evil works of the dead are not yet ended. The evils of Luther continue through the corruption of the minds of men with his books; and the glorious works of St. Paul still benefit men through his example and writings. St. Basil elegantly deduces this from those words of 1 Timothy 5:24: "Some men's sins are manifest, going before them to judgment; and some men they follow after" (*de Virginitate*). Thus, because bad as well as good works will come to an end at the same time as the world, so then the final sentence shall be imposed.

To the *second,* I say: There is no injustice because the soul enjoys beatitude without the body. Soul and body are not two substances such as are two companions, so that it would be an injury if one were rewarded before the other. Rather, they are one substance composed from two parts; moreover this one substance prefers that in the meantime one part of the two be ennobled rather than neither, and hence no injury is inflicted upon it, for an injury is not made willingly, but unwillingly. I say secondly, even if the soul and body were two substances, still no injury would be inflicted on the body when the soul alone is ennobled. The soul *principally* agrees to good and evil works, while the body only *instrumentally*. Nay more, no assent is made for merit and demerit except by the soul alone. Merit and demerit consist in the choice of the will, and such a choice proceeds from the soul alone, thus, they have their seat in the soul. I say *thirdly*, even if the soul and body equally make the principal assent to good and evil works, nevertheless, there would still be no injustice were the soul to be crowned before the day of judgment and not the body, because the disembodied soul has the capacity for glory and the crown, but the separated body has no capacity at all.

To the *third* I say two things. *Firstly*, the soul of Christ before the resurrection of his body did not ascend to a corporeal heaven, nevertheless, it was *formally* in the heavenly paradise, *i.e.* it was blessed and glorious. If our adversaries would attribute this to the souls of the saints, we would not be solicitous about that corporeal heaven. I say secondly, that Christ, in dying, resting, rising again, and ascending into heaven, was our exemplar in regard to the body; for we first die, second rest in the tomb, third will rise again, and lastly ascend into heaven corporally, just as Christ did. Moreover, that the soul of Christ descended to hell before it ascended into heaven does not pertain to the exemplar, for Christ did not descend into hell so that he would show us the way to hell, or that he would prepare a place for us there, rather, to lead the souls that were there out and destroy hell, lest thereafter the souls of the saints would be led there.

To the *fourth* argument, which is taken from the punishment of demons, I respond: many demons are not yet sunk into the abyss, but live in this our gloomy air to discipline men. This is why the Apostle calls them princes of this air (Ephesians 2:2). Just the same, all the demons are punished now, both with the punishment of loss (*poena damni*) and the punishment of sense (*poena sensus*). They are not better than men and still we have already shown the spirits of impious men weep in the punishments of hell, and on that account, since it is certain from the Gospel that the holy angels who stood in truth always see the face of God, why would it not also be a consequent that the rebel angels suffer the judgment of God? This is why Bede

Ch. VI: Arguments from Reason

rightly writes that the demons, though they fly to any place, everywhere they move is their hell (Epist. S. Jacobi, c. 3). And St. Augustine (*de corrept. et gratia*, 10) and St. Prosper (*de vita contmplativa*, 1) teach that the demons have already been judged and became miserable.

Nevertheless, there are many testimonies of the saints that seem to assert that the demons are not tormented with the penalty of hell before the day of judgment. Justin Martyr (*Apology*, 1 and 2), often repeats that demons will be handed over to eternal fire, but they have not yet been handed over. Irenaeus, (5, 23), says the devil never blasphemed God before the coming of Christ because he was still ignorant of his own damnation, but learned from Christ and the Apostles that the eternal fire has been prepared for him; the same Irenaeus shows he received that opinion from Justin. Oecumenius follows the same thing as Justin (on *1 Peter*). Epiphanius affirms, commenting on the heresy of the Sethians, that demons were not merely ignorant of their damnation, but also hoped for salvation through the coming of Christ. But when they saw that Christ did nothing for the demons, then at length they despaired of their salvation and began to blaspheme God through heretics.

St. Anthony, cited by Athanasius (*Life of St. Anthony*), said: "The demon is not ignorant of the torments that are coming and knows the fires of burning hell." Other fathers also have a similar opinion on the future torments of the demons, namely Ambrose (on Luke 8), Jerome and Chrysostom (on Matthew 8), Augustine (*City of God*, 8, 23 and *de nuptiis et concupisce*, 1, 22), Gregory (*Moralium* 4, 10 and *Dialog.* 4, 29), Theodoret (*epitome divinorum decretorum*, c. *de daemonibus*) and Bernard in his sermon on St. Malachy. But I do not see how we could defend the opinion of Justin, Irenaeus, Epiphanius and Oecumenius from error. The rest of the fathers affirm two specific things which are very true: on the day of judgment the demons will fall headlong from the air into the abyss and still they await future torments.

Moreover, it is not necessary to gather from this point, that they are not tormented at this time. For even if they are truly tortured and carry hell with them, as Bede says, nevertheless they will have the fullness of their punishments on the day of judgment when they are locked in the prisons of hell. They so fear the fulfillment of punishments that in exorcisms they seem to be tortured by no matter more than the menace of the coming judgment. This is the reason why exorcism prayers nearly always conclude: *Through him that is going to come to judge the living and the dead, and the world through fire.*

Furthermore, it seems they so fear that thrusting down into the abyss for these reasons: 1) Because they will no longer be able to harm men; 2) Because they will no longer twist away the worship due to God from anyone, as they do now while they are worshiped by the heathen and necromancers; 3) Because then their deceits, and weakness will be uncovered seeing that everyone shall know they are separated from men, women and children; 4) Because they will be judged not only by God but also by men, for we also judge the angels, as Paul witnesses (1 Corinthians 6:3).

CHAPTER VII
The Church Rightly Canonizes Saints.

NOW another question follows, which is on Canonization, and that is contained under four headings. *First*, we must explain whether saints may be canonized. Then, whose office it is to canonize. Then, whether the one who canonizes saints does so with an infallible judgment. Lastly, whether it is lawful to venerate[1] saints that have not yet been canonized.

Before we come to those chapters, we must briefly explain what canonization is. Canonization is nothing other than a public testimony of the Church on the true holiness and glory of some man that is already dead, and at the same time is a judgment and sentence whereby honors are decreed to him, which are due to those who reign happily with God. Such honors (as will be shown in the following disputation) are customarily seven.

1) Those who are canonized are inscribed in the Catalogue of the Saints, *i.e.* it is established and commanded that they are publically regarded as and called saints by all; 2) They are invoked in the public prayers of the Church; 3) Churches and altars are dedicated in their memory; 4) Sacrifices, both that of the Eucharist as well as praises and prayers, which are commonly called the *office* or the canonical hours, are offered publicly to God in their honor; 5) Feast days are celebrated in their honor; 6) Their

---

[1] Translator's note: The word used in Latin is *colere*, which generically means worship in this context. It is further distinguished between "worship" with *latria*, and "worship" with *dulia*. In modern English, however, "worship" means with *latria*, so it has been necessary for us to render the term *colere* as "venerate" when it applies to the saints, even though at times this produces some unevenness in the text.

images are painted, with the addition of a little quantity of light as a sign of the glory that they have in heaven; 7) Their relics are enclosed in precious receptacles and honored publicly.

Now that we have prefaced those points, we can prove that canonizing the saints is advantageous with the following arguments.

1) God himself willed sacred writers to record, in every detail, the glorious life and death of those who lived in their times, as is clear from Ecclesiasticus, who in chapter 44 canonized a great many saints, such as Enoch, Noah, Abraham, Isaac, Jacob, Moses, Aaron, Phineas, Joshua, Caleb, Samuel, David, Elijah, Elisha, etc. Likewise, in the New Testament, St. Luke canonized St. Stephen in the book of Acts, as well as James the Greater, and also Peter, Paul, Barnabas, Silas and others; therefore, it is trustworthy that God willed it to be done afterwards in the same mode.

2) We are held to honor and praise the saints both because Scripture commands it, "Let the people show forth their wisdom, and the church declare their praise" (*Sirach* 44:15), but also because their virtue merits this. For honor is, as it were, the natural reward of virtue, and at length, because it is advantageous for us to display the many benefits of their intercession. But unless we were to know who are true saints and who are not, we cannot venerate them as we ought.

3) It is proved by reason of imitation. The saints are certain examples of virtues, and norms of right living, and, as it were, a certain lamp enkindled before God so that they would give light to all others. This is why Paul says: "Remember your prelates who have spoken the word of God to you, whose faith you must follow, considering the end of their life" (Hebrews 13:7). But we cannot be

Ch. VII: The Church Rightly Canonizes Saints

enkindled to their imitation unless we know in particular whom we must imitate and what they did, or suffered. And the light ought to be placed on a lampstand, as it is done through canonization.

4) From the union which we have with them. In fact, we are members of one body, and members suffer compassion for each other as well as rejoice. So it is fitting for them to have compassion and be anxious for us, a thing that they do without a doubt even in particular, as well will teach below; and on the other hand, we rejoice in them and give thinks to God for their glory, which cannot be done without particular knowledge.

5) From perspective of unsuitability, for unless saints were proposed to our veneration for certain by a judgment of the Church, then it could easily happen that the people would often err and venerate damned men in place of saints, as happened in the time of St. Martin. For Sulpitius writes, that when the people venerated I know not which dead man as a martyr, and that practice was suspected by St. Martin because he had received nothing certain from the elders on that saint, at length, the soul of the man whom the people venerated in that place appeared to Martin while he was in prayer, and he confessed that he was damned for a certain theft, and he suffered the punishment of extreme torture for his crimes. The same happened in the time of Pope Alexander III, as is clear from c. *Audivimus, extra., de reliquiis et Sanctorum veneratione*, where he rebuked certain people who were accustomed to venerate a man that was slain while drunk as if he were a martyr.

CHAPTER VIII
Whose Office it Is to Canonize the Saints.

NOW we move to explain the second point: Who has the authority to canonize saints? We must note that someone may be canonized in two modes. In one mode particularly, so that a man is held to be and venerated as a saint in only one province or diocese. In the other mode, generally, so that he is held to be a saint in the whole Church, nor would it be lawful for anyone to have doubts about his sanctity.

In the *first* mode, any bishop could canonize, as Thomas Waldens teaches (*de Sacramentalibus*, tit. 4, 122) and it is clear from St. Cyprian (*Epist.* 3, 6) where he commands to be notified when some martyr passes from this life so that he could celebrate his memory with sacrifices right away, as well as venerate the day of his birth later. Then, it is also clear from many saints, whom, although certain provinces venerate them, they are altogether unknown in other provinces. This is why in the Council of Florence (sess. 7), the Latins say Symeon Metaphrastes is venerated as a saint in the Churches of the Greeks, but is unknown among the Latins. Nevertheless, though this was once permitted, it is no longer lawful since Alexander III and later Innocent III who, seeing abuses which arose in regard to the cult of the saints, forbade thereafter anyone from beginning to venerate someone as a saint without the approbation of the Roman Pontiff, as is clear from chapter 1 and 2 of *de reliquiis, et Sanctorum veneratione*.

In the *second mode*, to canonize, *i.e.* so that men shall be held as saints in the whole Church, according to the common opinion pertains to the Supreme Pontiff. For, it is held in cap. *Audivimus & Cum ex eo, de reliquiis et veneratione Sanctorum* and *Venerabili, de testibus et attestationibus*. And it is clear also from reason, for it is the scope of the one who is in charge of the whole Church to propose for it what must be believed and what must be done in matters which are of religion. Likewise from the contrary, to declare those who are heretics, so that they may be held as such by the whole Church, is for the Supreme Pontiff, as we have already shown; therefore, to declare who is really a saint and must be venerated belongs to the same supreme Pontiff.

Now, someone will say: There are many saints who are venerated in the whole Church that the Roman Pontiff did not canonize. For the first Pope (unless perhaps I am mistaken) who is read to have canonized saints seems to have been Pope Leo III, and St. Ludgerus writes an account of him in an epistle (*de miraculis sancti Suiberti*, c. 9 in 2. tomo Surii), "At length at the devout insistence of Charlemagne and Hildebald, Archbishop of Cologne, the same Pope came to Werdam from Cologne, and there after other solemnities for S. Suibert solemnly ascribed him in the Catalogue of holy confessors on 5 September." This is the first solemn canonization we read about, before which there might have also been others, but they are not proven. Later, Innocent II canonized St. Hugh, the bishop of Grenoble, as is clear from a letter of the same Pope given to the prior of the Carthusians, cited by Surius, tomus 2. From there, Alexander III reported St. Bernard among the saints, as is held at the end of the books on the life of the same Bernard, from which time all other saints, who are held as saints, such as St. Thomas Beckett, St. Dominic, St. Francis and others, were reported to be in the number of the saints by the Popes. Therefore, what shall we say about

Ch. VIII: Whose office it is to Canonize

so many saints who, before those times, were venerated in the Church?

I respond: Older saints began to be venerated in the universal Church not by some law, as it were, but by *custom*. Just as other customs have the force of law from the tacit consent of the prince, and without it they have no force (St. Thomas, I IIæ, q. 97 art. 3), so the cult of any saint that was introduced generally by the custom of the Churches, has its force from the tacit or express approval of the Supreme Pontiff.

CHAPTER IX
It must be Believed that the Pope Cannot Err in the Canonization of Saints

NOW we move to the *third* point, and there are two opinions on it. The first is of heretics, who hold that the Pope can err in canonization of the saints. So John Wycliffe, as Thomas Waldens relates (*de Sacramentalibus*, tom. 3, cap. 122) where he says the Pope can err no less in this matter than Prester John, the King of Ethiopia, or a Turk, or a Sultan. The Lutherans and Calvinists argue the same thing, seeing that in other similar matters they attribute no authority to the Pope.

The other is of Catholics, asserting that it is certain the Church does not err in the canonization of the saints, so much so that without any doubt, the saints canonized by the Church must be venerated. This is proven:

1) Because if it were lawful to doubt whether a canonized saint is really a saint, it would also be lawful to doubt whether he must be venerated; but this is false. In fact, St. Augustine (*epist. 118*) says that it is a most insolent insanity to dispute whether one may do what the whole Church does. We gather the same thing from St. Bernard, who in a letter to the canons of Lyons (*Epist.* 174), speaking about celebrating feasts in honor of the saints, says: "I securely hold and hand down what I have received from the Church." Besides, all the fathers venerated saints without any hesitation, and assert that they must be venerated. Lastly, we are held to obey the Pope when he appoints the feast day of some saint, just the same, we cannot do something against conscience, therefore, we cannot doubt whether a man who has been canonized by the Church may and must be venerated.

2) We prove it from two unsuitable consequents: in the first place, the saints are not deprived of the suffrage of the living since we are not allowed to pray for those who have been canonized, just as St. Augustine says (*Sermon 17*), while commenting on the words of the Apostle: "He that prays for a martyr does him an injury." And the same must be understood on all canonized saints, as Innocent teaches (c. *Cum Marthae, de celebrat. Missarum*). But if the Church could err in this it would defraud the man that is held as a saint and is not in fact, when no one prays for him. Next, the living would also be defrauded of the intercessions of the Saints; for if the Church could err in this they would often call upon the damned in place of the blessed. Besides, when the Church asks in the prayers for the feasts of the saints that just as God glorified them in heaven, he would likewise bestow grace upon us here on earth, it would pray for a curse in place of a blessing. And although it would not seek that curse, except materially, nevertheless, this whole thing looks absurd.

3) Great miracles that have been diligently examined make the matter evidently believable, as we have shown elsewhere. But saints are not ordinarily canonized by the Pope unless they are illuminated with great and certain miracles. And it is confirmed, for if we believe without any hesitation that Caesar and Pompey existed because we have it from the common consensus of historians, who themselves were men and could lie, why do we not believe without any hesitation that God himself witnesses the fact through miracles when there is no reason to suspect the contrary?

4) It is proved from the preparation. Before the saints are canonized, fasts and public prayers are appointed and the whole matter is very diligently examined for a long

Ch. IX: Infallibility of Canonizations

time; but it is not credible that God does not come to his Church, which is so disposed and begs for him to do so.

Lastly, it is proven *a posteriori*: because in other matters, in which the Popes can err, at some time errors get detected in that business; but in this no error has ever been detected.

But some object with a passage of St. Augustine: "Many bodies are honored on earth, whose souls are tortured in hell." *I respond:* This passage may not be a quote from Augustine, for I have never found it is his works. But whether it is or not, it can be understood to be about the impious, who are honored in very proud tombs, when still their souls are tortured in hell; or on the bodies of uncanonized saints; or on bodies that have been substituted for the bodies of saints; or at length, on the martyrs of the Donatists, who were honored by heretics as martyrs when really their souls were tortured in hell. See more on the argument of this point in St. Thomas (*Quodlibet.* 9, q. ult., art. ult.), St. Augustine of Ancona (*Summa, de potestate Ecclesiae*, q. 14 art. 4), John Driedo, *de Ecclesiastic. dogmatibus* 4, 1), St. Antoninus (*Summae Theologiae* 3. par. tit. 12 c. 8), Cajetan (*tractat. de ingulgentibus, ad Julium*, c. 8), Sylvester (*Canonizatio*), and Melchior Cano (*de Locis*, lib. 5, final chapter).

CHAPTER X
Uncanonized Saints may Be Venerated Privately, but not Publicly.

NOW we argue the fourth point, whether it is lawful to venerate uncanonized saints. I answer that it is lawful to have a *private cult*, not a public one, as the common opinion of the doctors that comment on *de reliquiis et veneratione Sanctorum*, cap. 1 & 2 confirms. In fact, the Supreme Pontiff, in that passage, forbids *public* cult, therefore it is reckoned on the contrary that he permits a private one. Moreover, when we say "public cult", we do not mean that it is displayed in the presence of others, but displayed the *name of the whole Church*, and as though the Church established it.

From what we understand, we must have a word on those seven types of honor that have already been enumerated in chapter 7.

1) As far as the first, it is lawful to believe an uncanonized man is a saint and call him such, still, not to preach him as though he were enrolled in the Catalogue of the Saints.

2) As far as the second, it is lawful to invoke an uncanonized man, even in the hearing of others, as is clear from Jerome in the life of Paula, and Gregory Nazianzen in the life of Athanasius and Basil; both invoked and praised them prior to canonization. Besides, we pray to the living, even if we do not know them to be saints, so why not the dead, when we trust upon greater reasoning that they are saints? But it would not be lawful to do this in public Litanies or in the divine office.

3) & 4) As far as the third & fourth, it does not seem lawful in any mode to relate those honors to uncanonized saints: for churches, altars and sacrifices are by their

nature of a public cult. For there is no sacrifice in the Church except the common one, and instituted by God himself. Moreover, churches and altars are assigned for sacrifice.

5) As far as the fifth, it is not lawful to celebrate a public feast. Nevertheless, it would be lawful on the day of a birth of an uncanonized saint to rejoice in a special way, as well as to free up time for God in their memory. The fathers also did this, and it can be seen from St. John Cassian (*Collat.* 19, 1).

6) As far as the sixth, it is lawful to paint and image and venerate it, but not set it up in a Church in the mode of other saints.

7) In regard to the seventh, it is not lawful to publicly constitute the relics of uncanonized men to be honored. Still, it is lawful to have them and venerate them in the sight of others, provided scandal is avoided; for the practice of the Church holds this. As soon as the martyrs were dead, the faithful ran to take up their relics. Similarly, when men die in the odor of sanctity, many devoutly kiss their hands and feet, and save their garments for relics; nor has this ever been forbidden. Besides, if it is lawful to honor living men whom we believe to be saints, why not the dead?

These few remarks should suffice for canonization. If someone desires to see more, let him read Augustine Triumphus in *Summa de Potestate Ecclesiae,* and Troilus Malvezius in his book *de Canonizatione.*

CHAPTER XI
A Question is Proposed on the Cult of the Saints, with the Arguments of our Adversaries.

NOW that we have concluded the questions on glory and canonization, the controversy on cult follows in right order. There was an ancient heresy cited by several of the Fathers, as well as some more recently, that held saints must not be venerated (the heresy of Eustachius, cited by Socrates, *hist.* 2, 33; that of Eunomius and Vigilantius cited by Jerome, of Claudius of Turin cited by Jona of Arles, and of Wycliffe cited by Thomas Waldens (t. 3, *de sacramentalibus*, titul. 13). In our own day, the Lutherans and Calvinists have again renewed it. The Lutheran Centuriators of Magdeburg (*Cent.* 1, lib. 2 cap. 4 col. 340) say all adoration of the saints is idolatrous. By equal reasoning, Calvin does not suffer any cult to be shown to the angels or holy men who are dead, no matter how small or great (*Inst.* lib. 1 cap. 11 §11, & cap. 12 § 1 & 2). These are Calvin's arguments:

1) Honor is twofold: one is civil, whereby we honor powerful, or wise men; the other pertains to religion, which is suitable to God alone; but that civil honor is not suitable for saints and angels, as we have already noted, since they do not live with us in civil society; but the honor of religion cannot be granted to them because religion is the worship of God. And with this distinction Calvin eludes Catholic arguments since he proves creatures can be adored after the example of Abraham, who adored the sons of Heth, and of James, who adored his brother Esau, and of the sons of Israel, who adored Joseph, for he would have it that all of these pertain to the civil cult.

2) If some religious cult were due to the saints, it would certainly be *dulia*, not *latria*, as Catholics teach. But it is

inept to say the saints are venerated without *latria*, seeing that worship means with *latria*, to worship without *latria* is to worship without worship. Then it is more δουλέιν than λατρέυειν, for δουλέιν is to serve whereas λατρέυειν is to worship, but to venerate someone is less than to serve them, for we venerate equals, such as friends and colleagues, but we do not serve them unless they are our masters.

This argument can be strengthened by Lorenzo Valla, and Theodore Beza, who in their annotations to Matthew 4, teach that *latria* and *dulia* mean the same thing, and are confused both in Scripture and among profane authors. In Leviticus 23:7 we read: "You will not do any servile work," which in Greek is always ἔργον λατρευτὸν οὐ ποίσετε. And on the other hand, in Romans 7:6: "That we might serve in the newness of the spirit," is in Greek: ὥστε δουλεύειν ἡμᾶς ἐν καινότητι πνεύματος. Therefore, *latria* is said to be on a work even in the use of men, and *dulia* on the worship of God. Likewise, in book 3 of *Cyropaedia*, Xenophon places λατρέυειν for the obedience of a handmaid toward her lord, and a little later the very same thing is called δουλέιν, which is why Augustine in q. 94 on Exodus says that both *latria* and *dulia* are attributed to God, *latria* as to God and *dulia* as to the Lord.

3) The next argument of Calvin is from the Scriptures. We read in Deuteronomy 6:13, "You will fear the Lord your God, and him alone will you serve." This is similar to that of Paul in 1 Tim. 1:17, "To God alone be honor and glory." Likewise in Matthew 4:10, although the devil does not call *latria* to mind, but only demands προσκύνησιν, that is a slight bow, the Lord rebukes him saying: "It is written, you will adore the Lord your God, and him alone will you serve." In that passage he shows that one cannot make any

Ch. XI: The Arguments of our Adversaries

bow to a creature for the sake of religion, otherwise it will pertain to idolatry. Likewise in Galatians 4:8, "you served them who by nature are not gods," in Greek is: ἐδουλεύσατε τοῖς φύσει μὴ οὖσιν θεοῖς. Therefore, *dulia* cannot be attributed except to one that is God by nature.

4) From the examples of the Scriptures: *(a)* In Ester 13:14, Mardochai refuses to bend himself in the presence of Aman. And when he gives an accounting, he says: "But I feared lest I should transfer the honor of my God to a man, and lest I should adore any one except my God." *(b)* Likewise in Acts 10:26, when Cornelius adores Peter, Peter forbade it saying: "Rise, I myself am also a man." Nor is it believable that either Aman meant to be adored as a God or that Cornelius wanted to adore Peter as God. *(c)* Likewise in Acts 14:14, Paul and Barnabas forbade the Lycaonians to venerate them. *(d)* Then, in Apocalypse 19:10, the angel said to John when he venerated him: "See to it that you do not do this, I am your fellow servant, etc. Worship God." And just the same, the angel was not ignorant that John showed him *dulia*, not *latria*.

5) From the Fathers. Athanasius (*Serm.* 3 against the Arians) teaches that we must not venerate holy men or angels in adoration. Epiphanius (*Panarion,* on the heresy of the Collyridianians) often repeats that Mary must not be adored, but God alone. Ambrose (on Romans 1) rebukes those who adore their fellow servants. Augustine (*de vera religione*, ca. 55) says: "The religious veneration of dead men is not for us, because if they lived piously then they would desire no honors, rather, they would want us to worship him in whose light they rejoice to be partakers of their merit." Further on he says the same on the cult of the Angels. Thus Calvin.

CHAPTER XII
The Catholic Teaching is Explained.

NOW the teaching of Catholics must be explained, on the matter that the theologians treat in *3 Sent.* dist. 9.

1) Moreover, we must *first* observe that three acts of adoration are embraced. *Firstly,* the act of the intellect, whereby we apprehend the excellence of something. *Secondly,* the act of the will whereby we are inclined inwardly to a thing and will to do something by an inward or outward act, whereby we profess its excellence and our subjection. *Thirdly,* the outward act, whereby we bow the head or bend the knee, or show some other sign of subjection. From the aforesaid acts the second is especially proper and essential; for the first act can be without adoration, while the third also with mockery.

2) In the *second* place, we must observe that there are as many species of adoration, or cult, as there are species of excellence, as St. Thomas teaches (II IIæ q. 103 art. 3). Honor, or cult, is due to a person on account of his *excellence*. But, because what was established pertains to the present, there are three species of excellence.

a) Divine and *infinite* excellence, to which the first species of cult corresponds, which the theologians call *latria*.

b) Human excellence or *natural*, which is posited in human virtues, dignities, states of life, etc. The second species of cult corresponds to this, which can be called the *civil* cult, and a certain human observance, although this can be divided into many other species, as Aristotle teaches (*Ethicorum*, lib. 9 cap. 2), seeing that one honor is due to a father, another to a prince, another to a teacher, another to a wise or learned man, etc.

c) The third excellence is a type of *middle* between divine and human, such as grace, and the glory of the saints; for these are supernatural gifts and most excellent, and the third species of cult corresponds to this excellence, which theologians call *dulia*, and because among holy creatures the humanity of Christ, if it were considered apart, singularly excels on account of the union to the Word, and similarly the Blessed Virgin, as mother of the Son of God, so excels the other saints, that she can be called Lady, and our queen, which does not suit the other saints except very imperfectly; therefore, theologians divide this third species, which they call *dulia*, into *dulia* properly so called, and *hyperdulia*, attributing the former to the rest of the saints, the latter only to the humanity of Christ, and to his mother.

3) *In the third place*, we must observe that these three species of adoration are not univocal, but analogous. Just as an excellence is not spoken of univocally regarding the excellence of God and creatures, so the cult due on account of the excellence cannot be spoken of univocally about the cult of God and creatures.

4) *In the fourth place*, we must note that these very species of adoration are best distinguished insofar as they consider inward acts. *a)* The first species, *i.e.* latria, is the supreme submission, and inclination of the will with apprehension of God, as first principle and final end, and thus the supreme good; such adoration is suitable to God alone.

b) The second species, *i.e.* the civil cult, is by far a lesser inclination of the will, with apprehension of a certain human excellence.

c) The third species is a certain middle inclination of the will with apprehension of an excellence more than

Ch. XII: The Catholic Teaching on Veneratiing Saints

human and less than divine. As regards outward acts, it is not easy to distinguish the species of adorations; for nearly all outward acts are common to every adoration, *with the exception of sacrifice*, and those things assigned to it namely churches, altars and priests; for God willed this cult of sacrifice to be shown *to himself alone*, as St. Augustine teaches (*de civitate Dei*, 10, 4), as well as Theodoret (*ad Graecos*, lib. 8, which is on martyrs) and it is clear from Exodus 22:20: "He that sacrifices to gods, let him be put to death, save only the Lord." From other outward acts, which are common to the cult worship of God and the veneration of a creature, it cannot evidently be gathered whether someone gives worship due to God to creatures or not, for Abraham, in the same act of bending to the ground adored God in Genesis 17:3, angels in 18:2, and men in 23:7.

5) *In the fifth place*, we must observe that latria is now and again taken for the act itself, whereby God is worshiped; now and again for the habit whereby a man is rendered willing to worship God. Furthermore, this habit is a certain special, and moral virtue, as St. Thomas teaches (*3. Sent.* dist. 9, q. 1). Nor is what St. Augustine says opposed (*Enchiridion*, cap. 3 & 12, *de Trinitate*, c. 14), that the worship of God consists in faith, hope and charity. There, he seems to mean that latria is the general virtue inflamed by the three Theological Virtues. Just as charity, and prudence are special virtues, because they have a special object, and at length are at the same time general in some mode because they direct, or order the acts of every virtue; so latria is a special virtue on account of its special object, *i.e.* divine honor; nevertheless, it is at the same time general because it uses the acts of all virtues to honor God, and especially those of faith, hope and charity. Supreme honor is brought to God, since through faith we

profess him to be the first truth, through hope to be omnipotent, through charity to be the best. Therefore, the object of the act of faith itself is God; but the very act of faith is an object of religion, and therefore faith is a theological virtue because it exists in regard to God. Religion is not a theological virtue because it exists in regard to a creature. The same can be said about hope and charity; for the object of these virtues is God, but their acts can pertain to the object of religion.

6) *In the sixth place*, we must make an observation in respect to terms. In Hebrew there is no noun whereby the cult of God alone is properly outlined, rather everything is common and the same noun is in one place attributed to the cult of a creature, in another place denied to it, insofar as one and the other are received. The Greeks translated Deuteronomy 6:13 as: αὐτῷ μόνῳ λατρεύσεις, "Him alone will you serve," but in Hebrew, that is: ותוא דובעת (*ottho thahhabod*), but the word דבע (*hhabad*) is as common in Hebrew as *servire* in Latin. Likewise, in Exodus 20:5, *You will not adore them*, which in Greek is rendered ου ωροσκθνησεις, is in Hebrew: הוחתשת (*thischthachaveh*), and is placed in all places cited above, Genesis 17:3; 18:2; and 23:7, and elsewhere in any place that it is said men, or angels or God are worshiped. In the Latin language, we likewise do not have any word which is only used to speak of the worship of God, as St. Augustine notes in *de Civitate Dei* (10, 1), and so, the fact is the fathers in one place concede the terms of adoration and religion to creatures, and elsewhere reject them, insofar as they are received in differing ways.

St. Jerome, says against Vigilantius (*epist. ad Riparium*) that neither the angels, nor relics of martyrs nor any created thing can be worshiped or adored. And still he

Ch. XII: The Catholic Teaching on Veneratiing Saints

himself, in his epitaph to Paula, says at the end: "Farewell Paula, and assist your worshiper (*cultorem*) with prayers." Furthermore, in *Apologia contra Ruffinum* (lib. 2), he says: "Come O Bethlehem, cradle of the Lord, and the manger I have venerated." So also Augustine, (*de vera religione*, cap. 55) says the cult of religion is due neither to angels, nor holy men nor the dead, but to God alone. Nevertheless, in *contra Faustum* (20, 21), he says: "The Christian people celebrate the memories of the martyrs with religious solemnity."

Therefore, sometimes they received the name of religion and adoration as suited to the principal analogy, *i.e.* to that special virtue, which has for its object the worship of God and which is distinguished in species from that virtue whereby we venerate the saints; but sometimes they received it more broadly for everything in that virtue, whereby we either worship God or venerate the friends of God, and other sacred matters, and it is distinguished from the political and merely human cult. In the Greek language there is one proper term for the worship of God, namely Θεοσεβεια, which is not used very much. Apart from that term there are four others, ἐυσεβεια, *piety*, θρησκεια, *religion*, then λατρεια and δουλεια, service; but all of these are at some time also attributed to creatures.

Now, although these terms are not proper to divine cult, according to the first institution of these words, nevertheless the schoolmen devised this distinction between latria and dulia, and not without reason. For, seeing that *in re* a manifest distinction is found between the cult of God and the saints, it is also necessary to find distinct words so as to avoid an equivocation. Moreover these two were the best. 1) Because the sacred writers never take up the term λατρεια, except for the worship *of*

God alone, which is clear from the whole New Testament. Yet they take up the term δουλεια, for every service, both of God and men. Nor is it opposed that in the Greek version of Leviticus it once uses the word latria for human service, for the Hebrew text and the Latin vulgate have the most common term, which is accommodated to every service. Then, the ancient fathers never attribute the word latria to any except for God, although still, they also say the saints are venerated, as is clear from Augustine (*de Civitate Dei*, 10, 1 and contra Faustum, 20, 21) and from all the Fathers of the second Council of Nicaea, as is seen in acts 3, 4, 6 & 8, and still more from John Damascene (*orat. 1 & 3 de imaginibus*), as well as Jona of Arles (*de cultu imaginum*, lib. 1), Bede (on Luke 4). Nay more, all the fathers called the cult of false gods *idolatry*, not *idolodulia*, because they saw the cult proper to God, according to the ecclesiastical manner of speech, was called latria, not dulia, as Augustine notes (*Questions on Genesis*, 61).

Nor is it opposed that these Fathers rarely mention dulia by name. When they say the saints and images ought to be venerated not with latria, they show clearly enough that they ought to be venerated with another species of cult; we call it *dulia*, just as Bede calls it in chapter 4 of Luke, and St. Peter Lombard with all the schoolmen (*3 Sent.* dist. 9). And St. Augustine insinuates the same thing in *City of God* (10, 1) where he says the cult due to a creature is not called latria by St. Paul in Ephesians 6, rather by another name, which the Apostle there calls dulia. Thus, there was no need, as Martin Peresius said (*de traditionibus*, part. 3 *consideratione* 7) to offer much proof that the name of dulia was taken for the cult of the saints, since dulia properly shows service, and we are not servants of the saints, but fellow servants. For in Scripture dulia is

Ch. XII: The Catholic Teaching on Veneratiing Saints

not only taken for the service of slaves, but also for *honorary subjection* as in Galatians 5:13: διὰ τῆς ἀγάπης δουλεύετε ἀλλήλοις, "serve each other in charity". So in this mode the theologians could call the cult of the saints dulia.

CHAPTER XIII
The Catholic Teaching is Asserted by Argumentation.

It now remains that we prove some cult, less than divine and greater than civil and merely human is due to sacred things, holy angels, and holy men.

1) The first argument is taken from Psalm 98 [99]:5, *Adore his footstool, for it is holy.* There, literally the footstool for the feet of the Lord is understood to be the Ark of the Covenant. In 1 Chronicles 28:2, David says: "I thought to build a house in which the ark of the covenant of the Lord and the footstool of our God might rest." It is not without reason that the Ark was called the footstool of the Lord; for above the Ark was the *propitatorium*, as it were the seat of God, which was held in the hands of two cherubim, which is spoken of in the beginning of this Psalm, in verse 1: "He that sits on the cherubim, let the earth be moved, etc." The same thing is found in Psalm 131 [132]:7, in these words: "We will go into his tabernacle; we will adore in the place where his feet stood." In Hebrew it is: "We will worship his footstool." And it is clear that it speaks about the Ark, because of what precedes it: "We will go into his tabernacle." And immediately after it follows: "Arise O Lord, into your resting place, you and the Ark which you sanctified." And this same thing is gathered more clearly from 2 Kings [Samuel] 6:2, "The ark of God, upon which the name of the Lord of hosts is invoked, who sits upon the cherubim."

But now, that some worship is commanded in these places is clear from the word *adorate*, because even in Hebrew it is the proper word of adoration, והשתחו (*isthachavu*). Moreover, that the ark is a created thing there can be no doubt, because then that cult would not be civil, but religious, as is clear from the argument of David: "Because it is holy," namely, this footstool. For civil cult is due to things on account of a civil and human excellence, but it is said the ark is adored not on account of a civil excellence, but because it is sacred and holy, since it is the footstool of God.

Bucer and Calvin respond in their commentary on this passage of the Psalm, that temple is understood for footstool. Moreover the command is not that the temple be adored, but that God would be adored in the temple, and they offer two proofs. *First*, from the Hebrew word להדם (*lahadom*) for footstool; *secondly*, from the verse: "Because it is holy," seeing that in Hebrew קדוש (*kadosch*) is ambiguous, but the Septuagint explained it when it rendered it ἅγιος not ἅγιον.[1]

I respond: by the word "footstool," the ark is necessarily understood as we have already shown, and hence the exposition of the heretics comes to ruin. The ark is not a place in which the Jews can enter to worship God. Then, even if the footstool were the temple, still our argument would win out, because David does not say worship "in the footstool" but worship the footstool, and it is proved. Firstly because the Syriac renders it: "Bend your knee to the temple." Likewise the Septuagint and Jerome render it: "Adore the footstool."

Secondly, because in nearly every place of Scripture we have where something is worshiped, the construction is with a ל (lamed), as in Genesis 23:7, "Abraham adored the people of the earth," *i.e.* the sons of Chetch. ויקם אברהם

---

[1] Translator's note: The difference is in the gender. By using ἅγιος, Bucer and Calvin argue, since it is masculine, it cannot be referring to footstool which is neuter.

Ch. XIII: Argumentaiton for the Catholic Teaching

תח־ינבל ץראה־םעל וחתשיו (*Vaiisthachu lahham haarets libne chet*).

Thirdly, because even if it were rendered: to the temple, still it would mean the same thing, for the Hebrew word means: *Bend your knee to that thing.*

Fourthly, because Jerome, in his epistle to Marcella where he urged her to move to Bethlehem, witnesses the ark itself was customarily worshiped: "Certain Jews worshiped the holy of holies, because there were cherubim, and the *propitiatorium*, and the ark of the covenant, etc." And the same thing is shown from other Scriptures, namely Joshua 3:4, 1 Kings [Samuel] 6:19, 2 Kings [Samuel] 6:7, Hebrews 9:7. In Joshua 3:4, while journeying they are commanded never to come within two thousand cubits of the ark. In 1 Kings 6:19 the Bethsamites, because they saw the ark without due reverence were slain by God, at least 50,000 men. In 2 Kings 6:7, the Lord killed Oza in a similar fashion when he touched the ark, which was not allowed to anyone but the priests. Lastly, on account of the honor of the ark, no man could enter the holy of holies where it was, except the high priest once a year, as Paul teaches in Hebrews 9:7. But certainly the ark was a created thing, and that honor shown to it did not proceed from urbanity, but some *religion*.

Now, we turn to their argument on the verse, *Because it is holy*. I affirm it is not translated incorrectly. The Septuagint and St. Jerome translate it the same way. But this is nothing *ad rem*, for whether it says the footstool must be adored because it is holy, or because it is of the holy God, the purpose of religious adoration is always advanced.

2) The Catholic teaching is proven from adoration shown to angels by pious and prudent men. In Genesis

18:2, Abraham, while prostrate on the earth, adored an angel. And Lot did likewise in Genesis 19:1. Now, since the response could be made that both Abraham and Lot did not think they were angels, but thought they were men from the beginning when they adored them, and only adored them with civil cult, we offer clearer passages. Numbers 22:31: "The Lord opened the eyes of Balaam, and he saw the angel standing in the way with a drawn sword, and falling flat on the ground he worshipped him." Here certainly he adored him no earlier than at the point where he knew it was an angel; moreover it would be ridiculous to say that civil honor is due to the angels. Likewise, in Joshua 5:13, when Joshua saw a man standing with an unsheathed sword, he said: "Are you one of ours, or our adversaries?" And the angel said in v. 14: "By no means, but I am the prince of the host of the Lord and now I am come. Immediately, Joshua fell on his face and worshiped." Here, obviously we see that middle adoration which we seek: for the fact is Joshua did not reckon the one he worshiped to be God, as is clear, because the angel said he is the minister of God. But he also did not worship him civilly, rather *religiously*, as is clear, because he did not adore him any earlier than when he understood it was an angel of God. That he did not act wickedly by adoration is clear, because the angel did not only not forbid him from adoration, but also commanded him to show him still greater honor, saying: "Take off the shoes from your feet, for the place where you stand is holy." Furthermore, that place was not holy except on account of the presence of the angel, for then Joshua was not in a sacred place, but in the plains of Jericho.

3) It is proven from the adoration of the saints in the Scriptures. In 1 Kings 28:14, Saul venerated the soul of

Ch. XIII: Argumentaiton for the Catholic Teaching

Samuel when it appeared to him. Moreover, it is certain that civil honor is not fitting for the souls of the dead, nor can it be said in this that Saul erred, seeing that neither Samuel himself, nor the Scripture rebukes Saul. Likewise in 3 Kings 18:7, Abdias, a holy man, adores Elijah prostrate on the ground; nor can we say this was civil cult, for as far as human excellence is concerned, Abdias was greater than Elijah, for the latter was a private man, but he was one of the princes of the king. Therefore, he adored him as *prophet*, and a man of God made excellent by a singular holiness. Likewise, 4 Kings 2:15, the sons of the prophets, when they heard the spirit of Elijah had come to rest upon Elisha, approached and adored him while prostrate.

Lastly, Daniel 2:46. Nebuchadnezzar worshiped Daniel. Now, who would say or believe that a captive, such as Daniel was, would be worshipped by a supreme king with civil honor? Therefore, he adored him religiously, as *a man filled with God*, nor did he adore him through an error, thinking him to be a god, for adoring him he said in verse 47: "Truly your God is the God of gods, and Lord of kings, and a revealer of hidden things, seeing you could discover this secret." But even the king of Alexandria did this to the priest Jaddo, as Josephus writes (*Antiquities* lib. 11 cap. 8).

Nor is it opposed that Nebuchadnezzar commanded sacrifice to be offered to Daniel. Scripture does not say that sacrifice was due to God alone, for the Sacrifice proper to God is immolation of animals, in Hebrew חבז (*zebach*), which is spoken of in Exodus 22:19, "Let he that immolates to gods be killed, apart from the Lord alone." There, the word in Hebrew is חבוז (*Tsobeach*), but Nebuchadnezzar did not offer חבז (*zebach*) to Daniel, but החנמ (*mincha*), and ויחוחינ (*nichochin*), this is gifts and incense, both of which are customarily offered to God and men. In 1 Kings 10:27

we read of certain Israelites that did not wish to recognize Saul as king, nor confer gifts upon him, and the word used there for gift is הַמִּנְחָה (*mincha*). Moreover, we also offer sweet odors in the very Church to images, and relics, although still, we assert, sacrifice must be offered to none but God alone. Nay more Dionysius (*Eccles. hierarch.* part. 2 cap. 3), says that a bishop, where he begins to burn incense during the sacred mysteries, first incenses the altar, then he does so around the whole Church, which we see is done even now. If this is not pleasing, then let us say with Jerome, and Theodoret, that Nebuchadnezzar offered sacrifice to Daniel, *i.e.* to the God of Daniel.

4) The fourth argument is taken from the confession of the Fathers, who lived from ancient times even to our own. Justin Martyr, (*Apolog.* 1, 6) speaking in the name of all Christians, and explaining the faith of the whole Church, says: "But we venerate him [God the Father] and his son who came and taught us these things, and others following him, and similarly the army of good angels, and we worship and adore the prophetic spirit in word and deed, and truth; and that to all who wish to learn, we fully pass on these things, even as we were taught and prepared."

Origen (*homil.* 3 *in diversos*), says: "Their memory is always celebrated in the Church, as is fitting."

Eusebius (*praeparat. Evangel.* 13, 7), says: "We practice it daily, for we honor the soldiers of true piety, as great friends of God." The same Eusebius, in (*hist.* 4, 15), relates from the epistle of the Church of Smyrna, on the martyrdom of St. Polycarp, that although the gentiles feared lest Christians, leaving Christ behind, might adore Polycarp, the older Christians said they could not in any way worship martyrs for Christ, but still loved them and

Ch. XIII: Argumentaiton for the Catholic Teaching

venerated them, because they preserved the faith intact with teacher and Lord.

Athanasius (*de Virginitate*,[1] near the end), says: "If a just man will enter your house, with fear and trembling run and worship on the ground at his feet." And, to show he spoke about religious worship, he says in the same book: "For, you do not worship him but God, who sends him; for the Lord says he who receives a just man, receives me." Note there, that God is adored in the just, not because adoration will not be restricted to the just man, but because God is the reason why the just man is adored. Just the same, it is said that he who receives a just man with hospitality, and gives him alms, receives Christ and gives him alms, because it is done *for the sake of Christ*, and Christ so receives it as if it were done for himself.

St. Basil, in an oration on St. Mamantis, says: "The Church urges on those in this life by the fact that she honors those who went before them." And in his oration on the forty martyrs, he says: "The honor, which we show to our good fellow servants of itself offers the sign of good will to our common Lord."

St. Gregory Nazianzen, in his oration on the Maccabees, asks why the holy Maccabees are not venerated everywhere as is due to them from their martyrdom. And in an oration against Julian the Apostate (4, 27), not far from the beginning, he spoke about a time

---

[1] Translator's note: In Bellarmine's time, *De Virginitate* was attributed to St. Athanasius and the authorship was not disputed. Today, however, it is accepted to have been falsely attributed to Athanasius and comes from a Syriac text which, in turn, is thought to be a translation of a Greek original written sometime between the 5th and 9th centuries.

when Julian the Apostate gave honor to a certain martyr, and that martyr refused with a marvelous sign: "O unexpected miracle! O brotherly love of the Martyrs! They did not accept honor from him that was hereafter to do dishonor so many martyrs!" And a little after he had said that the honor of the martyrs is a special mark of love in Christ.

St. Gregory of Nyssa in his oration on Theodore the martyr, where he said many things on the cult which is shown to the martyrs by the Church, says: "What king has been shown such honor? Who from them, who only seem to excel men in a manner, is celebrated with such a memorial? What emperor was sung and celebrated with such report, as this poor soldier, a conscript, Tyro, whom Paul armed, whom the angels anointed, whom Christ crowned?"

St. Epiphanius (*Panarion, haeres.* 79), refutes the error of those who offered sacrifice to Mary as though she were a goddess, fearing lest on that occasion no honor would be shown to Blessed Mary, as is the case with heretics today, and he most wisely repeated those words: "Where Mary is held in honor, the Lord is adored."

St. John Chrysostom (hom. *de sanctis Juventino et Maximo*), says: "You do not venerate on the one hand more ancient saints, and on the other more recent ones, but all of them with the same ardor. ... And the martyrs whom we venerate today, they adore. ... This is why we often visit them, adore their tombs, etc."

St. Cyril of Alexandria (*In Julianum*, lib. 6), says: "We do not say the holy martyrs became gods, but customarily deem them worthy of all honor."

Theodoret (*ad Graecos*, lib. 8) says: "For our Lord has brought his dead into the place of your gods, whom he has utterly abolished and has given their honor to the martyrs, etc." There it must be noted that the honor of gods is given over to the martyrs, because where the gods were worshiped, now the martyrs are venerated, but not in the same mode. For Theodoret adds: "But we, O Greek men, do not run down with sacrifices nor any drink offerings, rather we honor them as holy men and beloved friends of God."

Then, St. John Damascene (*de fide Orthodoxa*, 4, 16) says: "It is proper to honor the saints as friends of Christ, as sons and heirs of God, etc."

From the Latins, Tertullian calls to mind the celebration of feasts on the birthday of the martyrs (*de Corona militis*).

St. Cyprian (4, epist. 5) says: "We celebrate the passions of the martyrs and their [birth] days with annual commemoration."

St. Ambrose (serm. 6), "Whomever honors the martyrs honors Christ also, and he that despises the saints, despises the Lord."

St. Maximus (serm. *de natali sanctorum Octavii, Aventoris, et Solutoris, Martyrum*), says: "All the martyrs must be very devoutly venerated, but especially those whose relics we possess."

Prudentius says on St. Hippolytus: "Whenever I bowed in prayer here, a sick man diseased in soul and body both, I gained help." Note: *I bowed in prayer.*

Paulinus, in the first *Carmen* on the birth of St. Felix: "Rome, possessing the altars of St. Peter and St. Paul, rejoiced to open out in honor of this God, etc."

And on the eighth *Carmen*: "In whose honor God rejoices, because the martyr had contempt for his own honor."

St. Jerome (in epist. ad Riparium), says: "We honor the servants so that their honor would redound to the Lord." And in the life of Paula, he says: "Farewell, O Paula, and help your worshiper with your prayers." And in the same book he says that Paula, when she visited the holy hermits, customarily lay prostrate at the feet of each so that she might venerate them, as if she worshiped Christ in each of them. There, certainly she did not act according to a civil cult, for a noble woman would not civilly honor country people with such a sign of subjection.

St. Augustine (serm. 1 *de Sanctis Petro et Paulo*), says: "The multitude of the nations adores the most blessed Peter the fisherman on bended knee." And in his commentary on Psalm 44 [45] he says: "Show me at Rome a temple of Romulus held in so great honor as I can show you the memory of Peter is. Who is honored in Peter except he that died for us?" The same thing in book 20, *Contra Faustum*, c. 21, to the objection of Faustus, that Christians turn idols into martyrs, he answers that Christians venerate martyrs, but not with latria. And in Psalm 96, when the heathen objected that Christians worshiped angels, he answers likewise, and adds: "Would that you will also venerate them; for you will easily learn from them not to worship them, that is, not to worship them as gods, but as saints."

St. Gregory (*Dialog.* 3, 24) says that St. Peter appeared to a certain Theodore while he was hanging lamps in a Church dedicated to Peter himself, so that he might show that he approves of the veneration which they showed in serving him.

St. Bernard, in his sermon on the verse, *A great sign*, etc., says: "They embraced the footprints of Mary and with devout supplication laid prostrate before her blessed feet."

Ch. XIII: Argumentaiton for the Catholic Teaching

And in the following sermon, which is *de Aquae Ductu*, he says: "We venerate Mary with all the innermost marrow of the heart, with all the affections of the soul, and all devotion, because this is his will, who wills us to have the whole through Mary."

5) The fifth argument can be taken from the invocation in churches, feasts, devotions, pilgrimages, images, and other things, from which it follows: there can be no doubt that all of these pertain to the cult of the saints.

6) The sixth argument is from the fact that the heathens, Jews, and heretics always accused Christians of idolatry on account of the cult of the saints; but certainly they would not have done this unless they saw that Christians religiously venerated the saints. The Fathers witness this about the heathen, namely Eusebius (*hist. de Judaeis*, 8, 6 and in *de Juliano Apostata* 4, 15); Cyril (*in Julian. de Manichaeis* 5 and 10) Augustine (*contra Faustum* 20, 21; *on Prophyry, Vigilantius, and Eunomius*), and Jerome against Vigilantius.

7) The seventh argument is taken from reason. If civil honor is due by reason of civil virtue, wisdom, power, and nobility, then an honor that is more than civil is due by reason of supernatural virtue, wisdom, power and nobility. Yet the saints, with respect to supernatural virtues, altogether excel since they burn with divine charity and cannot sin; for nothing stained can enter the kingdom of heaven (Apocalypse 21:27). With respect to wisdom, they see uncreated wisdom itself, and see in it the causes of all things, according to that of Matthew 5:8, *Blessed are the pure in heart, for they will see God*. With respect to power, they are kings of heaven and partakers of that very divine throne, as it is said in Apocalypse 21:3, *He that will conquer, I will give to him a seat with me in my throne*. And

in Luke 22:29, *And I allot the kingdom for you just as my father has allotted it for me.* With respect to nobility, they are sons of God, now by real adoption confirmed by glory. Therefore, duly and rightly they must be pursued with the best religious cult.

Lastly, God promised honor and glory to the saints: "He that will have glorified me, I will glorify him" (1 Kings [Samuel] 2:30); "He that will have ministered to me, my Father will honor him" (John 12:26); and "Glory, and honor, and peace to everyone working good" (Romans 2:10). Consequently, honor is due to them, and certainly not from anyone other than us, who are inferior to them. Civil honor is not suitable for the dead, therefore, religious honor is due to them.

CHAPTER XIV
The Arguments Proposed Previously Are Answered.

NOW let us briefly refute the arguments of our adversaries.[1]

1) If Calvin understands the cult *of latria* by the cult of religion, we affirm the saints ought not be worshiped with the cult of religion; but we deny that apart from the cult of latria there is no other cult but civil. For we have already shown that there is a third cult, which is also of religion albeit *secondarily*.

2) I admit the cult of dulia is due to the saints and I deny it to be absurd. Now, I answer the *first* proof: to venerate without latria is not to worship without cult, but to worship without a certain type of cult. For, St. Augustine, who was not inept I should think, says the saints are venerated, and not with latria (*Contra Faustum*, 20, 21).

To the *second* proof, I say: Dulia is not more than latria, for according to profane authors they mean the same thing; moreover, according to Scripture and the use of the Church latria is greater than dulia by far. For, latria is not any worship you like, but the cult *of the highest service*; dulia is a cult *of any service you like.*

Now, someone will say: But we are not servants of the saints, but fellow servants; therefore dulia is not fitting for the saints. Some would answer that the cult of the saints is not called dulia, that is servitude, because it is shown to them by servants, but because it is shown by those who are servants of God. But they feared where there was no fear.

So it must be said that dulia means any particular service, both perfect and imperfect. Furthermore, perfect

---

[1] In Chapter XI.

service pertaining to those things which are, are referred to another and the motion is caused by another, both the efficient and the final cause, that is, they are done for the sake of the Lord and are moved by the Lord as instruments to performing some action, as Aristotle teaches (*Polit.* l. 1, cap. 3). Imperfect service is of those who have some of these qualities, but not all of them, that is, who are moved by some other mode. This is why, an infant is said to differ in no way from a servant, even if he is a lord (Galatians 4:1), because he is moved by another agent as an efficient cause. On the other hand, a man that rules, is said to be the servant of those whom he rules, according to what is said in 2 Corinthians 4:5, "We ourselves are your servants through Jesus," because he is moved by another agent as a final cause. So, even if we are not perfectly servants of the saints, still we are so *imperfectly*, insofar as they move us, and help us to do good works by their example and intercession with the Lord. Hence St. Paulinus always calls himself the slave and servant of St. Felix (*Natal.* 1, 2 &3), and St. Gregory did not fear to say to Peter, his interlocutor, that the solicitude of servants was pleasing to God.

Now, to the confirmation from Valla and Beza; I affirm that according to the use of profane writers dulia and latria are the same, nevertheless, according to the use of Scripture, latria is almost never received for the cult shown to a creature, and according to the use of the Church, altogether never. And, just as the ancient Church was allowed to devise new terms against the heretics, such as ὁμοούσιος, why would the Church not be allowed at a later date to devise some new terms against later heretics, or certainly to use the same terms with a different meaning?

Ch. XIV: Previous Arguments are Answered

Now I respond to that of Augustine on dulia and latria with respect to God. That passage favors our position, for in it, when Augustine says latria is given to God as God, and dulia to the same as he is Lord, it is gathered that latria cannot be imparted to a creature since there is only one God. But dulia can be imparted because truly there are many that are also properly lords, while at the same time we affirm that dulia, whereby God is worshiped, is a dulia through an excellence and is distinguished in species from that whereby the saints are venerated.

3) Now for the third argument. *First*, I say, that the passage of Deuteronomy 6:13, *You will worship the Lord your God, and him alone shall you serve*, is about that service which is suitable for God alone. In Greek the word is λατρεύσεις, wherefore, Augustine remarked in q. 61 on Genesis, that it was not said you will worship God alone and him alone will you serve, but: "You will worship God and him alone will you serve." Here, worship is also suitable to creatures, but not the service of latria, which is described here. Besides, although it was written to him alone δουλευσις, it should be explained in the same mode, namely, you will serve him alone with a certain, specific kind of service, but not absolutely will you serve him alone. Accordingly, in the Hebrew text it is הובעת [thahhaboth] and still we find, not withstanding this precept, it was said of Jacob by Isaac, "Let the people serve you and worship the sons of your mother" (Genesis 27:29). There the words are דבע [havad] and וחתשי [istachavu]. Besides, just as we read here, *him alone will you serve*, so we also read in 1 Timothy 6:16 "Who alone has immortality," and yet we know that angels and souls are immortal in their own specific mode.

Now to that of 1 Timothy 1:17, *To God alone be honor and glory*, I respond: This must likewise be understood in regard to a certain honor and glory, for in Romans 2:10 we read: "Glory and honor and peace to every one that works good." Lastly, it is said more narrowly in Isaiah 44:6 "I am first, and I am last, and besides me there is no God," yet we still read in Psalm 81 [82]:6, "I said you are gods," nevertheless, the first is not false, but must be understand in a sound manner.

I say to that of Matthew 4:10 that the devil demanded from Christ προσκύνησιν as a sign of latria, and hence demanded latria. For that reason, the Lord answered him: "You will worship the Lord your God, and him alone shall you serve."

To the verse of Galatians 4:8, *You served* [ἐδουλεύσατε] *those who are not gods*, I respond: the verb δουλευειν is common for service of God and of creatures, and so it should be explained according to the exigencies of the place. Here, it is taken for the worship of God alone, since the circumstances of the passage necessarily demand it.

4) To the *fourth* argument. I say: a) Aman wanted to be worshiped as a god, and this is the very thing we gather from the words of Mardochai.

b) In regard to Cornelius, I say with St. Jerome (*Contra Vigilantium*), that Cornelius thought some divinity resided in Peter, and therefore was rightly corrected. Or, with Chrysostom on this passage of Acts, that Cornelius piously venerated Peter, but the latter refused this honor out of modesty although it would otherwise be due to him.

c) What a wonder if Paul refused sacrifice to be offered to himself? For we said above that it is an external act due to God alone.

Ch. XIV: Previous Arguments are Answered

d) I say: This passage favors us; for John thought the one that appeared to him was God, or an angel. If God he was rightly rebuked; if an angel, and still he venerated, why are we rebuked who do what John did? Do the Calvinists know better than John whether angels must be venerated?

But why, they ask, was he rebuked? *Firstly*, because perhaps the Angel appeared in such a way that he could be mistaken for Christ. For he said in Apocalypse 1:17, "I am first and last, and was dead, and behold now I live, etc." Therefore, he could have been mistaken for Christ, whose person he managed, unless he explained that he was not Christ and therefore John was corrected not on account of an error of adoration, but on account of the error of person. Augustine answers in this way (q. 61 in Genesis).

Secondly, I say that John rightly meant to show cult due to an angel, just as he recalled that Abraham, Lot and other of his fathers had done; still the angel forbade it on account of reverence for the humanity of Christ. Now, before the arrival of Christ the angels suffered themselves to be venerated by men; but after God became man, and all the angels began to worship the man in Christ, they refused to be venerated by men, especially by the Apostles and other great men. So think Bede, Anselm, Richard, Rupert in their commentaries on Apocalypse 19, as well as the *scholia Graeca* in ch. 22, and before these authors St. Gregory (*Moral.* 27, 11; *hom. 8 in Evang.*). Nevertheless, it does not follow that we act wrongly if we adore angels, for we rightly adore them, and they rightly refuse to be adored. Therefore, John himself, when in chapter 19 he heard once, "See lest you do this, etc." still in chapter 22 willed again to venerate the same angel. He understood that he acted rightly by venerating and the angel acted rightly in refusing, but one may not suppose that John was either forgetful or indocile.

From the fathers, I say they spoke against the errors of the pagans who turned wicked men into true gods, and offered them sacrifice. In six hundred places the same fathers affirm that holy angels and men must otherwise be attended with due cult, many of which we already related above.

CHAPTER XV
The Controversy on the Invocation of the Saints is Proposed.

WE have proven that the saints must be venerated. Yet, because there is a peculiar difficulty on the cult of invocation, thus it now falls in right order that we treat on the invocation of the saints.

There are two extreme errors on this question; the truth is in the mean, as it usually is. 1) The *first* error is that the Blessed Virgin Mary, who is special among the saints, may and must be invoked no differently than God. Formerly some whom St. Epiphanius relates and refutes (*Panarion, haeres.* 78 & 79) so thought. The *second* error is that none of the saints should be invoked after death in any way, because the dead cannot pray for the living; or if they can, they only pray in general because they cannot hear the prayers which we pour forth to them. This error is of many.

First of all, it seems Vigilantius was the first to dash his foot upon this stone. Yet Alonso de Castro (*de haeresibus*, v. *Sancti*) attributes this error to Eustathius, who lived before Vigilantius, but it cannot easily be proven. In fact, Eustathius scorned the basilicas of the martyrs and perhaps also their relics, but he taught nothing on invocation. See Socrates (2, 33) and the Council of Gangrense. Consequently, Vigilantius, as we find in St. Jerome's work against Vigilantius, taught that after death nobody hears prayers for another, and consequently, dead saints do not pray for the living, from which it follows that they are called upon in vain.

Then, the Henricians, or Petrobrusians, and Apostolics clearly and boldly opposed the invocation of the saints in the time of Bernard, as the saint himself relates (serm. 66

in Cantica) as well as his anonymous biographer (*vita S. Bernardi*, 3, 5). Later the Waldensians taught the same thing (St. Antoninus, 4 par. tit. 11 ca. 7 § 2). Juan Torquemada witnesses that a man by the name of Cathar taught the same thing (*summae de Ecclesia*, lib. 4 part. 2 cap. 35). John Wycliff taught the same thing (as Thomas Waldens writes, tom. 3 tit. 12, cap. 108 et seq.), and also the Taborites who are of the family of Jan Huss, as Aeneas Sylvius writes (*de orig. Bohemor.* cap. 35). Although Wycliffe did not say it was illicit to pray to the saints, he taught it was merely useless and superfluous. Furthermore, he said it seemed like foolishness to have recourse to the clowns of some prince when the prince himself is most prepared to hear you himself, or to follow turbulent rivers when the fountain itself is open. By such words, he compared in passing the saints to clowns and turbulent rivers, which is what we would expect from heretics.

Lastly, this error is held by the heretics of our time, such as Luther (in *libris ad Waldenses*); Melanchthon (*Apologia* art. 21 *Confess. Augustanae*); Brenz (*Confess. Wirtemb.* cap. 24) and Calvin (*Instit.* lib. 1 cap. 14 § 12 and Lib. 3 *Instit.* c. 20 § 20 et seq.). They teach three things on the prayers of the saints. 1) That dead saints pray for the living is not contained in the Bible, and hence this is not certain; 2) If the saints pray, they do not pray except in general for the whole Church of the elect, but not for this or that person in particular; 3) It is useless and illicit to call upon the saints or angels, or men and ask that they would pray for us; useless because they do not have ears long enough (as Calvin says) to hear our prayers; but illicit because by this the glory of Christ is obscured, who is our sole mediator and intercessor.

CHAPTER XVI
Some Frauds and Lies of the Heretics Are Detected

THUS, now we have the teaching of our adversaries; but before we refute it, it will be useful to become acquainted with the calumnies and lies of Melanchthon as well as Calvin, with which they persuade simple-minded men.

Melanchthon (*loc. cit.*) gives three lies. *Firstly*, that we attribute divinity to the saints, *i.e.* the power of knowing the thoughts of men. This is clearly a lie, for no Catholic has ever said that we assert such a thing. For we assert they know our prayers not as they are in our minds, but as they are in God, whom they see and who shows such to them.

Secondly, before the times of St. Gregory, no mention of invocation of the saints exists. Martin Chemnitz (*Examen Concil. Tridentini*, sess. 22) was more generous, who says the invocation of the saints began after the times of Augustine, and later (*ibid*, sess. 25), says the author of the invocation of the Blessed Virgin Mary was Peter Gnapheus, who lived around the year 480. Now such inexperience or malice is intolerable in so many teachers in Israel, since there are innumerable citations in Ambrose, Augustine, Jerome, Basil, Athanasius, Irenaeus and others, whom we are about to cite, and which are even cited by the Centuriators (*Cent.* 4, c. 4, and Cent. 5, c. 4).

Thirdly, that Papists are asses because they teach from the book of St. Jerome against Vigilantius, and that Vigilantius denied the invocation of the saints, seeing that in that whole book of Jerome there is not one syllable on the invocation of the Saints, but only on the honor of relics. But this very statement shows that Melanchthon, while certainly not an ass, was certainly very stupid; for even if Vigilantius did not say the saints must not be invoked, nevertheless, he said "they cannot pray for us". Moreover, if we were not to gather from this that he denied the invocation of saints, then truly we would be slower than asses. The reason is, who would invoke someone that cannot offer any help? Thus, the Centuriators act more wisely (*Centur.* 4, cap. 8) who, seeing that it cannot be denied that Vigilantius supposed the same thing which they do, they say that he was not a heretic, rather a holy priest and he contended with St. Jerome and won.

Next, Calvin says many marvelous things. *Firstly*, he upholds that in the hymns and litanies of papists there is no mention made of Christ, and since we always pray to dead saints, we never hasten to Christ in prayer (*Instit.* lib. 3 cap. 20 §21). Yet, this is certainly such a lie that there is a danger that the devil might lose his title of "liar". Don't we say in the litanies, *Lord have mercy, Christ have mercy, Father the God of heaven,* etc.? Are not all the hymns which we read in the breviary either from Ambrose, or Gregory, Prudentius, or Sedulius, the most ancient of all authors? And are not all directed to God, and do they not finish with *Glory to you O Lord,* or something similar? Are not all the prayers of the Church that are read in the Mass directed also to God, and do they not terminate in *through Christ our Lord?*

Secondly, in book 3 ch. 20, he calls the saints reigning with Christ dead, skeletons, shadows, corpses, which is an incredible blasphemy.

Thirdly, he says Christ alone entered into the sanctuary of heaven, and he alone bears the prayers of the people standing afar in the hall (lib. 3 c. 20 §20). With such words he means that not only holy men, but even the angels cannot offer our prayers to God, but Christ alone, which is

Ch. XVI: The Lies of the Heretics

clearly against the Scripture. In Tobit 12:12, he says: "I offered your prayer to the Lord." and Apocalypse 8:4, "And the smoke of the incense of the prayers of the saints ascended up before God from the hand of the angel." And against Calvin himself, who forgot that he admitted angels offer our prayers to God.

Fourthly, he says (lib. 3 cap. 20 § 22) that we invoke the saints clearly as gods and that we have so many saints, not for the number of cities, as Jeremiah said of the Jews (Jeremiah 2:28) but for the number of the heads of the multitude; which is a manifest calumny as it appears from the litanies. For who would dare to say to God, "Saint God, pray for us?" Nor is that a new calumny, seeing that even the ancient enemies of the Church used to mendaciously declare that Catholics hold dead men for gods, as is clear from Cyril (*in Julianum*, 6, & 10), as well as from Eusebius (*hist.* 4, 15, and 8, 6), Augustine (*contra Faustum*, 22, 4) and Jerome (*contra Vigilantium*).

Fifthly, he says we ask the Virgin that she would bid her son to do what we ask (*ibid.*). But who on our side says this? Why does he not prove it by some example? Besides, if in Joshua 10:14 it is said: "While the Lord obeyed the voice of a man," why could it not be said in some fashion that the Son of God submits to something that his mother asks for?

Sixthly, he says we mutter the *Pater Noster* in front of statues of Barbara or Catherine, and pastors approve of this usage with their applause (*ibid.*) But even the most simple-minded of the faithful, if they were asked, would usually respond that they direct the Lords' prayer to God, because if they do so in the presence of images of the saints, that hope for their help will cause their prayers to come to God better and more happily. But even if someone were so stupid that he would say *Pater Noster* to St. Barbara, should the ignorance of some be exhibited as though it were an ecclesiastical dogma? And who are the pastors who approve of this abuse?

Seventhly, he says that in the third Council of Carthage it was forbidden to say in public prayers "St. Peter, pray for us." Yet, that decree is not found in any place unless Calvin added it to the codex. For the Council only defined that the prayer of the priest offering the sacrifice be directed to the Father and not to the Son or the Holy Spirit, and no mention be made of saints. But Calvin, by his logic, because a prayer ought to be directed to the Father, he deduces the saints may not be invoked, and from there deduces further that the Council stated that it may not be said "St. Peter, pray for us."

Eighthly, he says that the sacrilege must be abhorred to call upon the saints as patrons of salvation, and what certain men say to the saints cannot be defended by any stripe; look upon us from heaven and help us. But the first words are of St. Ambrose in his book on Widows, the second part of St. Gregory Nazianzen in his oration on Cyprian, Athanasius and Basil. Moreover, antiquity has no one wiser than these two men.

CHAPTER XVII
How the Saints must Not Be Invoked

NOW, so that the truth of the matter would be made manifest, let us posit and prove some propositions.

1) The *first* proposition: *It is not permitted to ask the saints to concede to us glory or grace and other means to attain beatitude as though they were the authors of divine benefits.*

This is against the first error as well as the calumny of the Calvinists. It is proved: *a)* From Scripture: "The Lord will give glory and grace" (Psalm 83 [84]:12), and "I have lifted my eyes to the mountains, from where help shall come to me; my help is from the Lord who made heaven and earth" (Psalm 120 [121]:1-2). The mountains are holy men, as Augustine explains on this Psalm, and more profusely in other places (*Tract. in Joannem* 1; lib. *de Pastoribus*, c. 8). Therefore, we are bid to lift our eyes to the mountains, *i.e.* to the saints, and await help from them; but that we might understand that the help we expect from them is not from them as authors, but as those who obtain it. Thus we find next in verse 2: "My help is from the Lord who made heaven and earth". Likewise in James 1:17, "Every best gift, and every perfect gift, is from above, coming down from the Father of lights."

b) From the use of the Church; for in the prayers which are read at Mass, or in the office, or in the celebrations of the saints, we never asked for anything other than that the benefits of their prayers would be conceded to us.

c) For those things which we need are above the powers of a creature; and hence, even of the saints. Thus, we ought to ask nothing from the saints except that they would entreat God for the things most useful to us.

d) We see that St. Augustine (*Civit. Dei* 8, 27 and 22, 10), and Theodoret (*ad Graecos* lib. 8) teach precisely that the saints must not be invoked as gods but as those who can treat with God, which they wish to do.

e) Nevertheless, we must note that when we say that we ought not ask anything from the saints except that they might pray for us, we do not act from words, but from the sense of the words; for in regard to the words, it is lawful to say: "St. Peter, have mercy on me, save me, open the entrance of heaven for me," likewise, "give to me health of the body, give patience and fortitude to me," etc. provided we might understand "save me and have mercy on me" as *praying for me*; give this and that to me *with your prayers and merits*. St. Gregory Nazianzen speaks the same way in his oration on Cyprian, as well as on Basil, and many other fathers. Then, the universal Church, when it says to the Virgin in the hymn *Memento salutis Auctor*:

> Maria, Mother of grace,
> Sweet mother of mercy,
> You protect us from the enemy,
> And receive us in the hour of death.

And to the Apostles in the hymn *Exsultet coelum laudibus*:

> By whose decree
> All like or pine;
> To those sick in soul health resign
> And unto virtue us incline.

And just as the Apostle says of himself: "That I might save some from them," (Romans 11:14) and "That I might

Ch. XVII: How the Saints Are not Invoked

save all," not as God, but "by helping *with sermons and prayers, etc.*"

2) The *second* proposition: *The saints are not our immediate intercessors with God, but whatever they entreat from God for us they entreat through Christ.* Note: three persons can be considered when we pray to God: one of God himself, from whom we ask benefits; the other Christ through whose merits we desire these things be given us; third of him who asks the benefits through Christ. From these three persons the first cannot be attributed to the saints, as we have already shown; nor the second as we show now; but only the third.

Therefore, we invoke the saints for this purpose alone, that they might do that which we do, because they can do it better and more efficaciously than we; we and they do it together better than we alone. Now the conclusion is proven: Christ is the only one who reconciled the world to God, and who merited glory and grace for us, as well as everything necessary for salvation, as is clear in Colossians 1:19-20, "Because in him, it hath well pleased the Father, that all fullness should dwell; And through him to reconcile all things unto himself, making peace through the blood of his cross, both as to the things that are on earth, and the things that are in heaven. And 1 John 2:2, "He is the propitiation for our sins; and not for ours only, but also for those of the whole world."

And so from here Christ is called the door (John 10:7) and the way (John 14:6) because, as he says, "no man comes to the Father except through me." Hence, he also says "Ask in my name" (John 16:23). Thus, he is called the mediator of God and men (1 Tim. 2:5) and the advocate with the Father (1 John 2:1). Consequently, we can ask nothing of the saints except that they would intercede with

God, apply the merit of Christ for us, and through Christ we might obtain grace and glory.

Secondly it is proven from the words of the saints. Ambrose says: "He is our mouth, through which we speak to the Father: our eye, through which we see the Father; our right hand, through which we offer to the Father" (*de Isaac*, cap. 8). St. Augustine, explaining a verse in Psalm 108, *his prayer shall be made in sin,* says: "Prayer which is not made through Christ, not only does not erase sin, but is also itself a sin." St. Bernard (*serm. de B. Virgine*) says: "It behooves us to have a mediator with the mediator, nor is any more useful than Mary." With such words he teaches that Christ is the *immediate* intercessor, who entreats by himself, the saints *mediately,* who only entreat through Christ the *mediator.*

Thirdly, it is proven from the prayers of the Church. For all which concern the saints, have that form: "Grant unto us O God, by the intercession of Saint N., such a benefit, through Christ our Lord, Amen."

CHAPTER XVIII
The Saints Pray for Us.

THEREFORE, we have seen how the saints must not be invoked. Now, that we might understand how they must be invoked, we come to: 3) The *third* proposition: *The saints pray for us at least in general, according to the Scriptures.*

We take our proofs only from those Scriptures which treat on holy men. *a*) Jeremiah 15:1, "The Lord said to me, unless Moses and Samuel will stand in my presence, my soul is not near this people." So, Moses and Samuel could already be dead and customarily prayed for the Jewish people. Therefore, it is false that dead saints praying for the living is not found in Scripture.

Calvin responds to this in two ways. *Firstly*, the contrary could be gathered from this passage. When it is said: *Unless Moses and Samuel will stand in my presence*, namely to pray, it means they neither stood nor prayed. And if these notable prophets did not pray, how much less do others?

On the contrary: Because even if perhaps it were to mean they did not pray at that time because they understood the matter already to be desperate, still, it means they otherwise were in the habit to pray when they thought they were able to entreat, otherwise this utterance of God would be inept; for if anyone were to say: If my beast of burden will have prayed for you, he will entreat nothing, he would speak ineptly. Why? Because beasts of burden do not speak. And likewise if anyone will have said: If Cicero or Demosthenes were here, they would not persuade me, they would speak ineptly because the dead do not usually come. So therefore, God also (far be it) would speak ineptly when he says: "unless Moses and

Samuel will stand in my presence;" if they could not at all, or were not in the habit of treating with God. It would be one thing if Scripture were to say *If they stood*, by way of an impossible condition to mean if they were alive now and prayed. Yet it says: "if they will stand," and the Greek has ἐαν στῆ not ἐαν ἱστᾶ. And in Hebrew it is דומעי (*yahhamod*); if Moses *will* stand.[1]

Secondly, he answers that the sense of this passage is this: if now, two outstanding men will stand in my presence, of the quality that Moses and Samuel once were, still it will obtain nothing. But on the other hand we oppose the most serious authorities, Chrysostom (*Epistol. 1 ad Thess.* hom. 1), Jerome (on this passage of Jeremiah) as well as Gregory (*moral.* 9, 12) who teaches that God spoke about the true Moses and Samuel.

b) 2 Maccabees 15:12-13, where Judas saw Onias the priest in a certain vision, praying for the Jewish people. Calvin has no answer to give to this passage, except to declare that this book is not canonical. But we prove that it is canonical by an argument, which Calvin cannot reject if he wants agree with himself. He asserts against the invocation of the saints as his most powerful argument the testimony of the Third Council of Carthage, as we saw in the answer to the arguments in the last chapter. Now in that same Council, chapter 47, it says: "Likewise it is [this Council's pleasure] that nothing be read in the Church

---

[1] Translator's note: There is a grammatical gloss that is lost here in English. To make a statement employing an impossible condition for effect, such as: "if only he were here" (when he could not be) the subjunctive mood of the verb must be employed. But the Greek and Hebrew use the indicative mood, which means an impossible condition for effect could not be used in this verse.

Ch. XVIII: The Saints Pray for Us

under the name of Sacred Scripture apart from the canonical Scriptures; moreover, these are the canonical Scriptures, Genesis, Exodus, ... two books of Ezra, the two books of the Maccabees, etc." So, let Calvin either receive the books of the Maccabees as canonical and divine, or, let him not deter us from the invocation of the saints by the authority of this Council. Furthermore, it cannot be said that those fathers were wise in one matter and out of their minds in another.

c) Apocalypse 5:8, where it describes the 24 elders in heaven that laid prostrate before the throne of God, having golden phials full of ointments which are the prayers of the saints, Primasius, Richardus, and the *scholia Graeca* (cited by Oecumenius and Gagneus), while explaining this passage, say those prayers are the intercessions for the weakness of the infirm.

d) 2 Peter 1:15, "I will endeavor that even after my death you may often have occasion remember these things (namely what has been entrusted even in memory)." As the *Scholia Graeca* cited by Oecumenius explains, some fathers did not ineptly gather from this that the saints, after death, have care of the living. And although this may not be an evident argument, nevertheless it is *probable*.

e) Luke 16:27-28, where the rich man prays for his brethren; therefore, how much more do the just pray for the whole Church?

f) Apocalypse 6:10, the souls of the holy martyrs seek vindication before their killers with great clamor; therefore, how much more do they seek mercy for their brethren. Now, Brenz answers that these prayers must be understood figuratively; for the dead saints are said to shout out to the Lord because the prayers, which the living pour forth, still resound in the ears of God. On the other hand, the rich man, while he lived, did not pray for his brethren. The holy martyrs also, while they lived here did not ask to be vindicated by God from their persecutors, but rather more that he would forgive them. Therefore, the prayer, whereby they seek vindication is *new*. While they lived, because they could sin and there was danger that if they sought vengeance they might do so from cupidity, they did not seek it. But now they seek it eagerly, and with a life of justice, as Bede rightly explains.

g) Lastly, let us add that the Scriptures clearly teach the communion of the Church triumphant with the Church militant. In Hebrews 12:22, the Apostle says we approach the Church of the firstborn, who are in heaven, *i.e.* the citizens of it (Ephesians 2:19); in Galatians 4:26, he says Jerusalem is our mother, which is in heaven. In Colossians 1:18 and Ephesians 4:15, he says Christ is the head over all the Church, and certainly this does not exclude the heavenly Church: but this communion itself necessarily demands that the members are solicitous for each other and help one another; this is the nature of members living under one head, as the Apostle teaches (Romans 12:4 et seqq.; 1 Cor. 12:15 et seqq.). Hence it appears how what Calvin says would be so false, in the *Institutes* (3, cap. 30 §24), that God willed that there should be no commerce with dead saints, but only between them and us. Rather, how could this be true if we are one nation, one people, one body? See Augustine in *City of God* (20, 9), where he proves this very thing.

4) The *fourth* proposition: *The saints who rule with Christ pray for us not only in general but also in particular.*

a) It is proved *firstly* that the angels pray for us and have charge of us, even in particular, which is obvious from Tobit 12:12 and Zachariah 1:12, Apocalypse 8:3,

Ch. XVIII: The Saints Pray for Us

Daniel 10:11, Psalm 90:11 and Matthew 18:10. Therefore, how much more do the spirits of blessed men do it? *In the first place,* they lack nothing which the angels have, insofar as it pertains to this office, seeing that they are endowed with intelligence and will; are always present before God; love us very much, and at length, they are equal with the angels, as it is said in Luke 20:36. So, they have something apart from the angels, namely that they are members of the body of the Church, joined more to us than the angels are, and they have experienced our miseries and dangers, something the angels have not experienced.

Calvin answers that this argument would conclude the matter if we could show that the spirits of holy men act as the angels do in being in charge of men, guarding them and taking part in their affairs. For he supposes (as Vigilantius once did) that all the saints are in a certain hall, as though locked and free of guard, never to go out from there or to have any solicitude in our regard.

Moreover, we will easily show that the living faithful are not only ruled and governed by angels, but also by the spirits of blessed men.

Now let this be the *second* argument: Christ promised it in Apocalypse 2:26-27, when he said: "And to him that overcomes and who keeps my works unto the end, I will give authority over the nations. And he shall rule them with an iron rod, and like a clay vessel they shall be dashed to pieces." And in 3:12, "He who overcomes I will make a pillar in the temple of my God," and in verse 21: "He who overcomes I will permit to sit with me upon my throne; and I also have overcome and have sat with my Father on his throne." Here John speaks on the spirits of the dead, as is clear from the words of verse 26: "who keeps my works unto the end," he also speaks about the time before the resurrection, as is clear from what is said in verse 28, "he will rule with an iron rod." For to rule with an iron rod does not mean to punish, which will also take place after the resurrection; rather it means to rule with a *pastoral rod*, which will only be done before the resurrection; moreover, it is called an iron rod because it does not bend before injustice, as we read in Psalm 44: "the rod of uprightness," *i.e.* the most upright scepter, the scepter of your kingdom, and also eternal, since his kingdom will have no end. Moreover, the verse that follows: "and like a clay vessel they shall be dashed to pieces," does not mean men shall be destroyed, but sinners when Christ crushes and destroys sins, as Augustine explains (*in Psalm 2*), according to that of Acts 10:13, "Kill, and eat." The elect are either ruled or put to pasture with an iron rod, while the reprobate are like the clay vessels that are shattered.

Now, what it means to rule with an iron rod is clear, *firstly*, from the Hebrew word which David uses in Psalm 2:2, מעורת (*therohhem*), as well as the Greek word that John uses in these citations of the Apocalypse (2:27; 12:5; 19:15), which is ποιμανε ς, meaning you put to pasture, or *you will rule pastorally*.

Secondly, from what is said in Apocalypse 12:5, "And she brought forth a son who is to rule all the nations with an iron rod;" but Christ does not punish all nations, rather, he rules pastorally.

Thirdly, because John takes his words from Psalm 2:8, where it is said that Christ rules his whole inheritance with an iron rod, "Ask of me and I will give you the nations for your inheritance and the utmost parts of the earth for your possession. You will rule them with an iron rod, and shall break them into pieces like clay vessels." Yet,

Ch. XVIII: The Saints Pray for Us

we cannot suppose the whole Church is going to be destroyed by Christ.

Fourthly, because Hilary, Augustine, and Theodoret explain Psalm 2, and Primasius, Bede and Rupert explain Apocalypse 2 in such a manner. So, we have the spirits of blessed men, after death, and before the day of resurrection receive power over nations both to rule and to put them to pasture, and indeed to be pillars in the temple of God, *i.e.* to uphold the Church which Chrysostom teaches is properly suited to the holy Martyrs (*Sermo de Juventio et Maximo*) and at length, to sit in the in the throne of Christ, *i.e.* to preside with him over the whole world, and to rule and guide the Church.

The same thing is gathered from what we read in Matthew 24:46-47, "Blessed is that servant whom his master, when he comes, shall find so doing. Amen I say to you, he will set him over all his goods." The Church is the goods of the Lord, as Hilary teaches (and we read the same thing in his preface on the Apostles, which is one from nine of the most ancient, as Pope Pelagius II, who preceded St. Gregory, says in *epistol. 4 decretali*). In that preface, it is said: "As eternal shepherd, you will not desert your flock, but through your blessed apostles you guard it with continuous protection, so that they are governed by the same rulers, whom you constituted pastors to be in charge of the vicars over the same work." The fathers clearly teach that.

Basil, in his *Oration for the forty Martyrs*, says, "O unconquerable regiment, O universal guardians of the human race, those best of friends that have charge of us, etc.," And Gregory Nazianzen, in his oration on Cyprian: "You look upon us from on high, direct our speech and our life, and shepherd this holy sheepfold, even at the same time as the king, etc."

Hilary, commenting on Psalm 124, says: "Neither are there lacking watchmen to stand before the powers of the saints, nor the fortification of the angels."

Ambrose, *in Lucam*, lib. 8, says: "Just as the Angels have power over others, so also they that merit the life of the angels."

Likewise Leo the Great (*sermo 2 de anniversario suae assumptionis*), says: "Peter, now more fully and powerfully carries out those matters that were consigned to him, and carries out all the parts of his duties and cares, in the very one through whom he was glorified." And he teaches similar things in sermon 1 and 3. Likewise, Maximus, in his sermons on the martyrs of Tauricus, says: "There is familiarity between them and us, for they are always with us, they tarry with us, this is, they guard us while we live in body, and follow us after they have left their body."

Then, Theodoret, in his eighth book *ad Graecos*, says: "They who embark on a journey from some place abroad, seek martyrs as their companions on the way, or rather more their guides on the journey. Now, when they have returned safe and sound, they give thanks, confessing the benefits they have received."

b) The same is proven in the second place, from the testimonies of the Fathers. Cyprian (*Epistles*, 1, 1) says: "If anyone of us, by the swiftness of divine condescension, shall depart from here first, our love may continue in the presence of the Lord, and our prayers for our brethren and sisters not cease in the presence of the mercy of the Father."

St. Gregory Nazianzen (*Oratio 14*, which is on the death of his father Gregory), says: "Now he effects more for us by

Ch. XVIII: The Saints Pray for Us

prayer than he did before by doctrine, the nearer he is to God after he has laid aside his corporal bonds."

St. John Chrysostom (*Sermo de Juventio et Maximo*), says: "Just as soldiers showing their king the wounds they received in battle speak confidently unto him, so [these martyrs] carrying their severed heads in his presence, can obtain from the king of heaven whatsoever they wish."

St. Jerome proves this very conclusion from what he set forth in his book against Vigilantius in his letter to Paula on the death of Blaesilla: "She prays also for you. For me too, I feel sure, she makes intercession and asks God to pardon my sins."

St. Augustine (*de Baptismo*, 7, 1) says: "May Cyprian assist us with his prayers while we labor in the mortality of the flesh as in a dark cloud, so that if the Lord would grant it, we may imitate insofar as we can the good that was in him."

St. Leo (sermo 3 *de anniversario suae assumptionis*) says: "Which duty even now the pious pastor does without any doubt, and performs the mandate of the Lord, confirming us with exhortations and not ceasing to pray for us, that we not be overcome by any temptation." And again (*sermo 1 de SS. Petro et Paulo*), he says: "But as we have proved for ourselves, and our forefathers maintained, we believe, and are sure that, amid all the toils of this life, we must always be assisted in obtaining God's mercy by the prayers of special patrons." Let them add to these all the testimonies that we assert for the following conclusion: for those who say the saints must be invoked, without a doubt affirm they pray for us.

Lastly, it is proven from the apparitions of the saints who clearly witness that they pray for us, even in particular. Eusebius (*hist.* 6, 5) writes that St. Potamioena promised the executioner that when she arrived unto the Lord, she would obtain some good for him. Then, three days after her martyrdom, she appeared to the executioner in a dream and placed a crown upon his head, and a little later according to the prediction of the martyr, he was turned from an impious executioner into a pious martyr for Christ.

St. Augustine (*de Cura pro mortuis*, c. 19) says: "For not only by effects of benefits, but in the very beholding of men, it is certain that the confessor Felix appeared when the barbarians were attacking Nola, as we have heard not by uncertain rumors, but by sure witnesses." You can see many other testimonies of this sort cited by Basil in his oration on St. Mamante, Gregory Nazianzen in his first oration against Julianus, as well as in the oration on St. Caesarius; Gregory of Nyssa on the life of Gregory of Neocaesarea; Theodoret (*hist.* 5, 24); Evodius and Lucianus on the discovery and miracles of St. Stephen; Ambrose in his sermon on SS. Gervasius and Protasius, and serm. 90 on St. Agnes; Prudentius in his hymn on St. Fructuosus; Paulinus' eighth hymn on St. Felix, Sulpitius on the life of St. Martin. All of these authors lived a thousand years ago.

CHAPTER XIX
The Saints must Be Invoked

THE *fifth* and last proposition follows: *The living piously and usefully invoke saints, whether they are angels or men.* It is proved firstly from scripture, for in Genesis 48:16, Jacob so says, blessing the sons of Joseph: "May the angel, who delivered me from all evils, bless these children." Here, clearly, holy Jacob invoked an angel. Likewise in Job 5:1, "Call, if there is anyone who shall answer you, and turn to some of the saints." There, by the name of "saints" he understands angels, as St. Augustine explains in in chapter 19 of his *Annotations on Job*. He also reckons, in the verse *Have mercy upon me, my friends,* (Job 19:21), that angels are spoken of, according to what is said in chapter 33:23, "If there will have been an angel speaking for him, one from thousands, he will have mercy upon you, and say, 'free him'." Just as also in 15:15, when he says: "Behold, among his saints none are changeable." By the term, "saints" angels are understood, seeing that the same is contained in 4:18 with these words: "Behold, they that serve him are not stable, and in his angels he found wickedness." Although these words do not seem to convict the matter, because they are not of the very writer of the book, but of Eliphaz, a friend of Job, just the same, they convict because they show that at that time there was a custom of invoking the patronage of the holy angels.

Likewise in Exodus 32:13, Moses prays: Remember, O Lord, Abraham, Isaac, and Israel, your servants." Theodoret, commenting on this passage (q. 67 *in Exod.*), says that holy Moses, since he did not think he was sufficient to please God, also applied the patronage of the patriarchs. There we must note that before the arrival of Christ, the holy ones who died did not enter into heaven, nor did they see God, nor could they ordinarily discern the prayers of suppliants. Consequently, they did not have the custom in the old testament of saying "O Saint Abraham, pray for me," etc., rather, men of this time usually prayed to God and suborned the merits of the saints who had already died, so that their prayers might thereby be assisted.

Calvin responds, that assistance from the merits of the saints was not sought with words of this sort, rather, they only commemorated the covenant which God had made with the patriarchs to protect and help their posterity.

But this solution does not satisfy. The covenant of God and the justice of the saints are recalled together, as is clear from Psalm 131 [132]:1, "Remember, O Lord, David and all his meekness," and in verse 10: "For David your servant's sake, turn now away the face of your Christ." These words are of Solomon, praying to God through the merits of his father David, who had already died, just as it is certain from 2 Chronicles 6. This is why even in 3 Kings 15:4, it is said, "For David's sake our Lord his God gave him a lamp in Jerusalem that he might raise up his son after him, and establish Jerusalem, because David had done right in the eyes of our Lord." And in Daniel 3, "Do not take your mercy from us on account of your beloved Abraham, your servant Isaac, and Israel your holy one." And Moses (Exodus 34:7, Jeremiah 32) and others when they prayed to God, used to say: "O God, who keeps mercy over thousands, who love you," *i.e.* those who, on account of the justice of the fathers, you are often merciful to their sons, which was to implore the merits of the just elders; this is why even St. Augustine (1, 149 *in Exodum*), says: "We are advised that when we are cast down due to lack of merit, the merits of those who love God can lift us up."

Ch. XIX: The Saints Must Be Inovked

Chrysostom teaches the same thing (*hom. 42 in Gen.* and *27 in Matt.*).

Besides, in both the Old and the New Testament, we often read the living are invoked by the living; for in 1 Kings 7:8, the sons of Israel say to Samuel: "Cease not to cry out to our Lord God for us, so that he might save us from the hand of the Philistines." Likewise, in the last chapter of Job: "Go to my servant Job, he will pray for you." In Romans 15:30, St. Paul says: "I ask you, brethren, that you might assist me in your prayers for me to God."

He repeats the same thing in Ephesians 6:18-19, 1 Thessalonians 5:25, 2 Thessalonians 3:1, Colossians 4:3, and Hebrews 13:18. Therefore, it will also be permitted now to invoke the same holy men reigning with Christ. If it were not lawful now, is it because they refuse? This is not so, seeing that they are provided with greater charity than before, and (as Cyprian says in his sermon *On Mortality*), they are secure in their immortality and anxious for our safety. Is it because they are they unable? This is not so, because if they could when they were pilgrims in this life, how much more can they now in their own country? Is it because they do not know what we pray for? This is not so, because how would the angels know the conversion of sinners, for which there is such great rejoicing in heaven, as it is said in Luke 15:10? Thus, the saints know our prayers. At length, would it be an injury to God or Christ if one were to invoke someone other than he? This is not so, because then it would not be lawful to invoke the living.

Moreover, our adversaries could never answer this argument. Calvin merely responds that there is a different accounting for invocation of the living and the dead, because the living are all joined by the one intercession of

Christ for them, so they ask God for others, because they are members to each other, and because the Scripture calls on us to pray for one another (James 5:16), but this same thing cannot be said about the dead; for even they are members of the same Church and rest upon the one intercession of Christ; whatever they ask for us, they ask God through Christ.

Thirdly, it is proven from the Councils. In the first letter of the Bishops of Europe written to the emperor Leo, which took place after the Council of Chalcedon, it so says: "We place St. Proterius in the first place in the choir, and in the rank of the holy martyrs, and we beg mercy by his intercession and for God to have mercy." And in the second action of the Council of Chalcedon, the Fathers say: "Flavian lives after death, may the holy martyr pray for us." Then, in the 6th general Council, canon 7 from the recent publication, it is said: "God, the creator alone being adored, let the Christian invoke the saints, so that they might deign to make intercession for him with the divine majesty." Likewise, in the seventh general Council, (act. 6), the Council says: "With fear, let us do all things, begging the intercessions of the unstained Deipara, as well as all the holy angels and the saints." Likewise, in the Council of Girona (cap. 3), of Arles I (cap. 29), of Mainz under Charlemagne (c. 33), Toledo V (c. 1) and Toledo VI (c. 2), as well as the second Council of Braga (c. 9), litanies are appointed to be recited either for the three day period before the Ascension, or in other times. Furthermore, these Councils were nearly all celebrated before the first thousand years. We may add to these the deed of St. Gregory, who appointed litanies for times of plague (*Vita*, c. 42; Walafrid Strabo, c. 28).

Ch. XIX: The Saints Must Be Inovked

But perhaps our adversaries will object that what are here called *litanies* were only the *Kyrie eleyson, Christe eleyson*, etc., for the Greeks call that a litany, as is clear from St. Basil (*epist. 63*) and one may observe them in the liturgy of St. Basil himself, as well as that of St. John Chrysostom.

I respond: In the aforesaid Councils, what they call *litanies* contain the invocations of God and the saints, which is how we describe it today. In the first place, Strabo (*De rebus Ecclesiasticis*, c. 28), after explaining what a litany is, as it was meant by these councils, namely the first Council of Arles, he says it is an invocation of the saints. Then, litanies were described for the three day period before the Ascension, and they were not said while standing, but while walking around some place. Today we see the same time is kept and the same rite, so these are altogether the same litanies.

It is proved *fourthly* from the testimonies of the Greek and Latin Fathers. The first of the Greek Fathers is Dionysius the Areopagate (*Ecclesiast. hierarch.* c. 7), who says: "Certainly it would be the same thing if a man who, while the sun bestows its rays upon his healthy eyes, were to put out his own eyes, and seek to enjoy the solar light; so does he cling to impossible and superfluous expectations, who beseeches the intercession of holy men, and, by driving away the holy efforts natural to the same, plays truant from the most luminous and beneficent commandments, through heedlessness of the Divine gifts."

St. Irenaeus (*adversus haereses*, 5,19) says: "And if she [Eve] was seduced, that she might eschew God, this woman (Mary) was persuaded to obey God so that the Virgin Mary would become the advocate of the virgin Eve." What could be clearer?

St. Robert Bellarmine

Eusebius (*Praeparationis Evangelicae*, lib. 13), says: "These customs also may fitly be adopted on the death of those beloved of God, whom you would not do wrong in calling soldiers of the true religion. Hence comes also our custom of visiting their tombs, and offering our prayers beside them, and honoring their blessed souls, believing that we do this with good reason."

Athanasius, in his sermon on the Gospel of the Most Holy Mother of God, that is, *On the Annunciation*, says near the end, "Incline your ear [O Mary] to our prayers, and do not forget your people. ... We cry out to you, remember us O Most Holy Virgin. ... Intercede for us O mistress, lady, queen, and mother of God."

St. Basil (*oration in 40 Martyres*), says, "Anyone who is in time of trouble, let him fly to these [martyrs], who in turn rejoice, let them pray to them, first so that he may be delivered from evils, and in the second, that he may endure in joyful matters." He says the same thing on Psalm 33, on the verse: *The eyes of the Lord are upon the just and his ears upon their prayers*, "some of the holy spiritual powers [angels] and those which are about the heavenly places are called the eyes because they are entrusted with our guardianship, and others ears, because they receive our prayers."

St. Gregory Nazianzen (*Oratione in Cyprianum*), speaking about a certain holy virgin on an occasion when a pagan magician sought through a demon to defile her, he says Cyprian "asked the Virgin Mary to bring help to this Virgin during such a trial. ... The virgin conquered, the demon was bound." Gregory also calls upon Cyprian, just as he did at the end of his oration on St. Basil, and in the end of his oration on Athanasius, where he so says: "May you cast upon us from above a propitious glance, and

Ch. XIX: The Saints Must Be Inovked

conduct this holy people and us in peace; aid us through struggles, uphold us, or take us to you, and make us such as you are, though I have asked a great thing."

St. John Chrysostom, in homily 66 to the people, near the end, "For he that was clothed in purple, he comes prepared to embrace those tombs, and laying aside his office he stands prepared to pray to the saints so that they might intercede with God for him, and he who is encircled with a diadem prays to the carpenter of wood and the fisherman as protectors." He exhorts the same to supplication of the saints in *hom. 5 and 8 on Matthew*, hom. 43 *on Genesis*, homily 1 on *1 Thess.*, and his sermon on Juventius and Maximus, and in other places.

St. Gregory of Nyssa, in his oration on St. Theodore, says near the end, "Intercede and pray for your country with the King and Lord of all. We fear afflictions, we await dangers, the wicked barbarians are not far off, preparing war against us. Fight for us as a soldier, as a martyr use your freedom to speak for your fellow servants. ... Yet, if we needed greater prayer and support of your brother martyrs compel the whole chorus and together as one pray, call forth Peter, rouse Paul, and likewise John the Theologian, the beloved disciple."

St. Ephraim, in his sermons *On the Praises of the Holy Martyrs*, says, "We pray, O blessed Martyrs, who tasted torments in earnest for the Lord and savior, and for love of him from your own will, that you would deign to intervene with the Lord for us poor sinners, so that the grace of Christ would conquer in us."

St. Cyril of Jerusalem (*Catechesi 5, mystagogica*) says, "When we offer this sacrifice, we recall those who fell asleep before us, first of all the Patriarchs, Prophets,

Apostles and martyrs, so that God will take up our prayers with theirs."

Theodoret, in his history of the holy Fathers, so concludes their individual lives: "But I, coming to the end of this narration, ask and beseech that I might obtain divine help from their intercession." He has many similar things in his work *De invocatione Sanctorum*, lib. 8, ad Graecos, which is on the Martyrs.

St. John Damascene (*de fide*, 4, 16), says "From the time when He that is Himself life and the Author of life was reckoned among the dead, we do not call those dead who have fallen asleep in the hope of the resurrection and in faith of Him. For how could a dead body work miracles? How, therefore, are demons driven off by them, diseases dispelled, sick persons made well, the blind restored to sight, lepers purified, temptations and troubles overcome, and how does every good gift from the Father of lights come down through them to those who pray with sure faith?"

Theophylactus (*ad Hebraeos*, c. 11), says: "Already now, they have a pledge and token of honor [the saints in heaven], from where else would they have the power to be able to come to the aid of those invoking them? Why else would men have trust in their intercession?"

Now from the Latins. Pope St. Cornelius, in his first epistle on the translation of the bodies of the Apostles, says: "Praying to God and our Lord Jesus Christ to purge the stains of your sins by the intercession of his holy apostles."

St. Hilary, commenting on Psalm 129 [130], says: "The nature of God does not need the intercession of the angels, rather our weakness; they are sent on our account, who inherit salvation, since God knows everything that we do,

Ch. XIX: The Saints Must Be Inovked

rather, our infirmity needs the ministry of spiritual intercession to beg and pray." He says similar things on the intercession of the Apostles and prophets in his commentary on Psalm 124 [125].

St. Ambrose, in his book on widows, says: "The angels must be entreated on our behalf, since they have been to us as guards; the martyrs must be entreated, whose patronage we seem to claim for ourselves by the pledge, as it were, of their bodily remains. They can entreat for our sins, who, if they had any sins, washed them in their own blood; for they are the martyrs of God, our leaders, the beholders of our life and of our actions. Let us not be ashamed to take them as intercessors for our weakness, for they themselves knew the weaknesses of the body, even when they overcame."

He says the same thing in his commentary on Luke 10:21, "The martyrs, by the honorable prerogative of heavenly grace, obtain the place of deceased kings, nay more, kings become suppliants unto the martyrs and martyrs come to be their patrons."

St. Jerome, in his epitaph to Paula, says: "Farewell, O Paula, and help your worshiper in his old age with your prayers. Your faith and works join you to Christ, and being present with him, you obtain more easily what you ask."

St. Maximus, in his sermon on St. Agnes, says: "O holy virgin, who shines so bright in the eye of Christ, and are beautiful to the Son of God, and acceptable to all the angels and archangels, we beseech you with all the prayers that we are able to make, do be mindful of us to the end, that he who has rendered unto you the crown of all your labors, may grant unto us also, a pardon and forgiveness of our sins."

Ruffinus (*hist.* lib. 2 c. 33), says: "The Emperor Theodosius went in procession with the priests and the people to the oratories and chapels, and lying prostrate before the shrines and monuments of the apostles and martyrs, he asked help for himself from the faithful intercession of the saints."

Prudentius wrote many hymns on the saints in that same time period, in which he teaches they are invoked by the living. We advance a few examples. In his hymn on St. Lawrence, he says:

> What each supplicant asks you for,
> he gets the happy fulfillment;
> we pray, we ask, we lay our claim
> and nobody comes back sad.
> It seems that you are always at the disposal of all,
> and that in your fatherly charity
> you press to your heart your fellow citizens,
> and you fill them with your benefits.

Likewise in his hymn on St. Cassian:

> The martyr, you may be sure,
> hears with all favor every prayer,
> and fulfills those that he finds acceptable.

And again in his hymn on St. Hippolytus:

> I owe to Hippolytus, to whom our God, Christ,
> has given power to grant what one requests.

Next, St. Augustine (*tract. 84 in Joan.*), says: "For on these very grounds we do not commemorate them at that table in the same way, as we do others who now rest in

Ch. XIX: The Saints Must Be Inovked

peace, as if we should also pray for them, but rather that they should do so for us." Likewise, in *Sermon 17* on the words of the Apostle, he says: "Ecclesiastical discipline holds that the faithful know when they recite the martyrs in that place at the altar of God, there should be no prayer made for them there, rather they pray for the rest of the faithful departed. It is indeed an injury to pray for a martyr, to whose prayers we ought rather be commended." Likewise, in his book *On the care for the dead*, 4, he says: "I do not see what help they are to the dead save in this way: that upon recollection of the place in which the bodies of those whom they love have been deposited, they should commend them by prayer to those same Saints, who have taken them as patrons into their charge to aid them before the Lord."

St. Victor of Utica (*de perseq. Vvandalica*, lib. 3) says, "Succor us, O angels of God. Intercede, O patriarchs; pray, O holy prophets; succor us, O apostles, who are our advocates. You, especially, O blessed Peter, why are you silent in the necessities of your flock? You, O blessed apostle Paul, behold what the Arian Vandals do, and how your sons groan in captivity. O all you holy apostles, petition for us."

St. Fulgentius, in a sermon in praise of the Blessed Virgin Mary, says: "Therefore, the Virgin Mary received all courses of nature in Our Lord Jesus Christ so that she might come to the assistance of all women that fly unto her."

St. Leo the Great (ser. 5 *de Epiphania*), says: "Confirm the friendship with the holy angels and patriarchs, prophets, apostles and martyrs; join in their riches, seek to embrace their suffrage by imitation of them." See the same thing in his sermons on the anniversary of the assumption of his pontificate, and on the saints Peter and Paul, as well as on St. Laurence.

St. Gregory the Great (*Dialogues*, 2, 38), "Where the holy martyrs lie in their bodies, there is no doubt, Peter, but that they are able to work many miracles, yea and also do work infinite, to such as seek them with a pure mind. But for as much as simple people might have some doubt whether they be present, and do in those places hear their prayers where their bodies be not, it is necessary that they should in those places show greater miracles, where weak souls may be most in doubt of their presence. But he whose mind is fixed in God, has so much the greater merit of his faith in that he both knows that they rest not there in body, and yet be there present to hear our prayers."

St. Gregory of Tours (*de Gloria Martyrum*, 1, 94) says, "Most blessed Cyprian of Carthage, both a bishop and martyr, frequently furnishes safety to weak supplicants."

St. Bede (*in Cantica*, lib. 4), says, "But we more frequently seek a grotto of brick, *i.e.*, of holy angels or men, seeking their intercession for us with the mercy of the holy Creator. These are the safest and firmest protections of the holy Church." He has the same thing in his commentary on Matthew, lib. 3, on the verse *They did not answer him a word*, he says: "The suffrage of the saints must be sought so that they will pray for the Church."

St. Anselm (*de excellentia B. Virginis Mariae*), "We pray, O Lady, through the very grace whereby the holy and almighty God so exalted you and gave to you everything that is possible with him, so that you might ask and obtain it from him on our behalf, and that fullness of grace which you merited would so work in us that one day, the participation in this blessed reward might mercifully be bestowed upon us."

Ch. XIX: The Saints Must Be Inovked

St. Bernard (*De Laude Beatae Mariae Virginis*, hom. 2), "In dangers, in distress, in perplexities, think on Mary, call upon Mary. Let her not depart from your lips, let her not depart from your heart, and, that you may win the suffrage of her prayers, never depart from the example of her life. Following her, you will never go astray; when you implore her aid, you will never yield to despair. Thinking of her, you will not err, under her patronage you will never wander, beneath her protection you will not fear; she being your guide, you will not be weary. If she be your propitious star, you will arrive safely in port, and experience for your self the truth of the words, 'And the Virgin's name was Mary'."

From these thirty ancient and most learned Fathers only five are later than Gregory. Thus it appears what an absolute lie it is which Melanchthon writes, that before Gregory invocation of the saints was unknown.

Fifthly, it is proven from the miraculous deeds of St. Bernard against this heresy. For it is written in his life (3, 5) that when St. Bernard preached in Toulouse against this very heresy, while the crowd of the people offered loaves so that the holy man would bless them, he blessed them making the sign of the cross, with these words: "You will know in this that what we say is true, and what the heretics try to teach you is false, if the weak among you will taste these loaves, and obtain health." And when the Bishop of Chartres, who was present, said: "If they shall receive them in good faith, they will be healed", Bernard added: "I did not say this, but truly five tasted and were healed, so that you would know that we speak the truth and are true messengers of God." And the author of this biography added, "So vast a multitude of those suffering illness gained health from tasting this bread, that the story was told throughout the whole province."

Note, these very miracles were not done specifically to commend the merits of St. Bernard, since he clearly said that the sick would be healed if what he had preached was true. Now, lest it might be attributed to the faith and devotion of the people, he added that all who tasted the bread were healed, whether with or without faith, so that without a doubt the whole miracle would be related to that purpose, to confirm the truth. Therefore, since innumerable miracles took place to confirm our teaching, either it is true or else God was a witness of falsity.

Lastly, we add the endless miracles whereby the Saints most wisely proved that they hear the prayers of the living and not only can but want to help those who invoke them. One can see these miracles related in many authorities (the epistle of Nilus recited during the seventh Council, act 4; Theodoret, *hist.* 5, 24 and lib. 8 *ad Graecos*; Ambrose *serm. 90*, which is on St. Agnes; St. Augustine, *de Civitate Dei*, 22, 8; Gregory of Tours in *de Gloria Martyrum et Confessorum*; Gregory the Great, *Dialogues*, 3, 22-25; St. Bonaventure in the *Life of St. Francis*).

From these it can be gathered how utterly pathetic the responses that the heretics apply to these passages of the Fathers really are. The Centuriators of Magdeburg (*Cent.* 4, 4) speak very inconsistently, for in one place they acknowledge these are testimonies of the fathers, but say they erred, in another place they spitefully say that the works of such men are uncertain. But they do not otherwise offer any proof than that of Ambrose (*De Spiritu Sancto*, 3, 12) and Epiphanius (*Panarion, in haeresi Colliridianorum*), who say that God alone must be adored. Yet, they do not wish to draw attention to the fact that

Ch. XIX: The Saints Must Be Inovked

these Fathers speak on adoration, which is due to God alone, in which sense we also agree only God must be worshiped, whereby what we say duly corresponds, that the saints must not be invoked as gods, but as friends of God.

Next, Brenz (*Würtemburg Confession*, c. 24) tries to elude all of it with the figure of a prosopopeia.[1] He says that when the Fathers invoke the names of the dead in their sermons as if they were living it is customary, just as in speeches we speak of heaven, or earth, or dead men, whom we know for certain do not hear it. In the first place, this is a fiction if there ever was one. Even if this were admitted in the testimonies of Basil, Nazianzen, and of certain others, who invoke the saints in their preaching, nevertheless, it has no place in the testimonies of Dionysius, Irenaeus, Hilary, Ambrose, Chrysostom, Augustine, and others who either teach the saints must be invoked or relate that they are invoked by some. But we should not admit this in the testimonies of Basil, and Gregory, because it is clear that these fathers in the same place promise help for themselves and others from that invocation, as well as the miracles which followed. This sufficiently shows that it was not an empty prosopopeia, but that invocation of the saints is an efficacious petition.

Now, Calvin (*Institutes*, 3, 20) responds. The Fathers meant to forbid this superstition, but could not break the fury of the crowd, just as the third Council of Carthage shows in c. 23 where it forbids prayers to be poured forth at the altar to anyone other than the Father. Calvin means

---

[1] Translator's note: Prosopopeia is a rhetorical device where one speaks as if he were another person, literally personifying someone else to give another perspective to the argument.

to gather from this that the Fathers of that Council at least meant to stop anyone from profaning the mystery of the Lord's Supper by invocation of the dead. He finds confirmation from St. Augustine (*de Civitate Dei*, 22, 10) where he says the saints are not invoked by the priest offering the sacrifice.

But this is a very weak refuge for Calvin, seeing that the Fathers did not seek to forbid invocation of the saints, and it is clear from their very words, which we have already cited. There, as we say, they persuade, exhort and teach that the saints must be invoked, and they themselves everywhere invoke them, and in the Councils they celebrated they commanded the saints to be invoked. Nor do we have one word from the Council of Carthage on the invocation of saints, rather, they only commanded that the prayer of the priest offering the sacrifice be directed to the person of the Father, not the Son or the Holy Spirit. We also preserve this, although we sacrifice to the whole Trinity.

St. Augustine also merely teaches that in the very prayer where the sacrifice is offered, the saints must not be invoked, but God, to whom alone the sacrifice is offered. For, the fact is that in the very sacrifice we commemorate the memory of the martyrs and they are invoked so that they will pray for us, as the same St. Augustine precisely teaches (*Tract. in Joan.*, *84*, and *serm. 17* on the words of the Apostle) as well as St. Cyril (*Catech. 5 mystagogica*) as we cited above, and the same is clear from the liturgy of St. John Chrysostom, and of other fathers, for the saints are invoked in all of them.

CHAPTER XX
The Arguments of our Adversaries Are Answered

NOW it remains to propose the arguments of our adversaries and answer them.

1) The *first* argument. The invocation of the Saints results in an injury to God, since in Romans 10:14 it is said, "How then shall they invoke him, in whom they have not believed?" Therefore, he alone is invoked, in whom we believe, but we do not believe in any but God, therefore, either we invoke God alone, or we will make the saints gods.

To these they add to citations of the Fathers. St. Ambrose, commenting on the first chapter to the Romans,[1] says, "For shame, everywhere they customarily neglect God, saying with a miserable excuse, as it were: Through them they can go to God, just as if through state officials they may come to the king. Well now, is someone so mad or heedless of his salvation that he would claim the honor of a king for an official, when if some men were found to have so acted in this way, would they not rightly be condemned for high treason? And do they not think they are guilty who abandon the honor of God for a creature and, leaving God behind adore fellow servants as if there was anything more that could be reserved to God? At any rate, a man approaches the king by tribunes and officials because he is just a man, and does not know to whom he may entrust the state. But to stand before God (from whom

---

[1] Translator's note: This commentary was attributed to St. Ambrose through most of the middle ages, but identified by Erasmus as belonging to Ambrosiaster. Modern scholarship universally accepts that it was not by Ambrose, though questions the authorship of Ambrosiaster also.

nothing is hidden for he knows what all men deserve), there is no need of any to give suffrage but a devout mind."

Likewise, Theodoret (*ad Graecos*, lib. 8), says: "The Lord our God has introduced his own dead into the temples in the place of your gods, and those gods of yours he has caused to disappear, and their honors he has apportioned to these martyrs. Instead of your festivals of Pan and Diasiis, and Bacchus, and the sons of Jove, and others like them, there are celebrated the public solemnities of Peter, and Paul, and Thomas, Sergius, Marcellus, Leontius, Antonius, Maurice, and of the other holy martyrs." In these words Theodoret confesses that we hold saints in place of gods.

I respond: Just as it would not be an injury, but an honor for kings when their friends are honored and ambassadors are sent to them, so no injury is inflicted upon God, but rather an honor when the saints are honored not as gods, but as friends of God and are received as patrons in God's presence. Otherwise, one would also do God an injury when he demands prayers from the living, as Paul did in Romans 15:30 and other places, and the Centurion would have done an injury to Christ since he sought help from Christ personally but through elders of the Jews (Luke 7:6).

To the *first* citation, I say there, it is a question on invocation in which someone is invoked as God and the first author of goods. For he precedes the commentary with: "All who invoke the name of the Lord will be saved." I say besides, really just as one cannot invoke God as God when he does not believe in him, *i.e.* one who does not believe he is God and who, in his unbelief, does not hope in him or love him, so also he cannot invoke the saints as saints and friends of God who does not believe in them in

Ch. XX: The Opposing Arguments Are Answered

this mode, *i.e.* he does not believe there are saints nor hopes in them as in their patronage, nor loves them as such. Nor is the word *invocation* or *faith* attributed to God alone in the Scriptures. For in Genesis 48:16, Jacob says, "May my name be invoked upon them, the names also of my fathers Abraham, and Isaac, etc." Based on that passage St. Augustine (*Loquutionum de Genesi*, n. 200) teaches that invocation is not only for God, but also for men. And in his epistle to Philemon, the Apostle says: "I give thanks to my God, always remembering you in my prayers, hearing of your charity and faith which you have in our Lord Jesus, and toward all the saints." St. Jerome shows at length from that passage that faith should be held in the saints.

To the passage of Ambrose, I say he argues against the pagans, who worshiped the course of the stars, against whom the Apostle argues. This is why he also says they worship fellow servants, *i.e.* creatures, not otherwise besides God; just as a man that conveyed royal honors upon an official. Now what he adds at the end, "To stand before God there is no need of any to give suffrage", is understood on the side of God, as if one were to say God does not need interpreters, since he sees and understands all things by himself; nevertheless, on our side we need someone to give us suffrage or at least to be very useful, as the same Ambrose very clearly teaches in his book *on Widows*, as we showed above.

Now, someone will say, the pagans could give the same answer.

I respond: This is not the case, for they think the supreme God is not immediately accessible, nor can one come to him unless he do so through the cult of lesser powers, as clearly Theodoret teaches in his commentary on Colossians 1.

To the citation of Theodoret, I say he meant to show the glory of the gods was translated to the Martyrs, because the temples and feasts of the gods were preserved in the churches and feasts of the martyrs. Nevertheless their temples and feasts, which true religion permits, are such that we do not hold martyrs for gods, just as the pagans held Jove and his sons, but as holy men and friends of God, who especially help us by their examples, prayers and merits. We spoke more of this matter above.

2) The *second* argument. Invocation of the saints does an injury to Christ, for in 1 Timothy 2:5, it is said, "For there is one mediator of God and men, the man Christ Jesus." If therefore, he alone is mediator, then whoever adds to God through another does him an injury. This is why St. Augustine (*Contra Parmenianum*, 2, 8) says: "If John would say, 'This I have written unto you that you would not sin, and if you sin, you shall have me as your mediator before God, and I will entreat for your sins, as Parmenian in a certain place made the bishop a mediator between God and the people; what good and faithful Christian could abide him? Who would look upon him as the apostle of Christ, and not rather think him to be antichrist? ... Paul did not make himself a mediator between God and the people; but required that they pray one for another, being all the members of the body of Christ." Besides, in Colossians 2:18, it is said: "Let no man seduce you, willing in the humility and religion of angels, walking, etc." On such words Theodoret so wrote, "Those who defended the law also drew them to worship angels, saying that the law was given by them. And this error remained long in Phrygia and Pisidia. This is why a Council was called in Laodicea, the metropolitan see of Phyrigia, which forbade men to pray to angels by a law.

Ch. XX: The Opposing Arguments Are Answered

And at this day one can still see in those parts the oratory of St. Michael. They used this policy, pretending humility, they said that the God of the whole world was not to be seen nor approached, and so, we ought to reconcile the good will of God unto us by the angels."

I respond: No injury is made to Christ by the invocation of the saints, nor do we invoke the saints to act in place of Christ or to help Christ, but that they may help us, whereby we might obtain from Christ what we ask. And if the argument would be valid or even conclude the matter, then prayers could not be sought from the living, which nevertheless, even the heretics concede would be contrary to the Scriptures.

To the *first* citation, *I respond:* There are three reasons that Christ is said to be the one and only mediator. *a)* Because he alone was the mediator through the mode of redemption. Now we must note that there are three modes whereby one mediator reconciles two separate parties: in one way by declaring whether each sides seeks something just; in another way, by paying a creditor on behalf of a debtor; in a third, by beseeching the creditor to remit the debt.

The first mode, which is by declaring each side seeks something just, has no place between God and man, because it is certain that man offended God.

In the second mode, Christ alone is the mediator of God and man, and in this mode the Apostle speaks, as is clear from what he adds to that citation of 1 Timothy: "Who gave himself for our redemption. Next, because he also writes to Timothy, a bishop in Ephesus, in Asia, where the heresy of Simon flourished in that time, which introduced angels in place of Christ, which is why he drives home everywhere in his epistle to the Ephesians and

Colossians, who were peoples of Asia, that Christ is the head of the whole Church and through him alone the world was reconciled to God.

In the last mode, the saints can also be called mediators between God and those for whom they pray. There is no reason why we should be afraid to transfer the word "mediator" to the saints, just as we transfer to them the words "advocate" and "intercessor", which are attributed to Christ in Romans 8:34 and 1 John 2:1. For St. Gregory Nazianzen, in his oration to Gregory of Nyssa, calls the martyrs mediators between God, and us, and St. Cyril (*Thesauri*, 12, 10) says the prophets and apostles were all mediators. Moses himself (Deuteronomy 5:5) says of himself: "I was the intermediary and medium between the Lord and you in that time." The Apostle alludes to these words in Galatians 3:19, when he says the old law was ordained through the angels, "in the hand of a mediator," that is Moses, and in Hebrews 9:15 and 12:24, he calls Christ the mediator of the New Covenant, to make the distinction from Moses, who was the mediator of the Old Testament.

This allows us to answer the argument from the testimony of St. Augustine. Since the Donatists thought the grace of the sacrament depended upon the priest, to such an extent that a good priest would sanctify in conferring baptism, while a bad priest would pollute in conferring the sacrament, and hence they made the priest the mediator of redemption in a certain mode. Thus, St. Augustine teaches the people are safe whether a good or bad priest baptizes them, because Christ is the one mediator of God and mankind. The fact is Augustine would not deny the priest can be called a mediator by praying, which is certain

Ch. XX: The Opposing Arguments Are Answered

because in the same citation he says Christians act rightly when they commend one another to prayer.

b) The *second* reason why Christ is called the one mediator, is that Christ is not only a mediator by his office, whereby he reconciles God to mankind, but also by reason of nature since he is the medium between God and man, seeing that he is both God and man—the very thing which was necessary to reconcile man to God. Nearly all the Fathers provide this reasoning, such as Ambrose, Chrysostom, Theophylactus, Theodoret, Oecumenius and others that comment on this passage of Paul, as well as Epiphanius (*Panarion, in Ancorato*). St. Cyril (*de Thesauri*, 12, 10 and *de Trinitate*, 1) Hilary (*de Trinitate*, 9), Augustine (*de Civitate Dei*, 9, 17) and Fulgentius (*de fide ad Petrum*, ca. 2).

c) The *third* reason is that Christ alone is a mediator of all men to such an extent that he needs no mediator. The rest of the saints, even though they are mediators between God and us, seeing that they cause God to be well disposed to us by their prayers, just the same, they needed to be reconciled to God through Christ the mediator and even now, whatever they obtain for us they obtain from God through Christ. But Christ did not need any mediator for himself or for us, or he does need one but, as it is said in Hebrews 7:25, "He goes by himself to God, always living to make intercession for us."

St. Augustine follows this reasoning (*Contra Parmenianum*, 8), when he says: "All Christian men commend one another to their prayers, for whom no one intercedes, but for all he is the one and true mediator." And so it is clear that there is another solution to the argument from the words of St. Augustine, for he does not deny that the priest can be a mediator for the people in prayer;

except in that sense in which one is said to be a mediator between God and men, who intercedes for all and he needs no one who will intercede for himself, or who intercedes through him.

Yet, Calvin presses the attack with this citation of Augustine which says: "for whom no one steps in, but for all he is the one and true mediator". But the saints, through us, pray for us, and no man for them.

I respond: When St. Augustine says that Christ intercedes for us, he means to say Christ is the one whom all make intercession to, so that he is the mediator of all whether they pray for themselves or others. In this mode Christ intercedes now for St. Peter, not because he prays for his salvation, but because he intercedes for my salvation which St. Peter also asks. Otherwise, even the angels would be mediators in that mode, in which Christ is, for the angels pray for all and no man for them. But then they are not mediators in the mode in which Christ is, because they need Christ through whom they obtain benefits from God for us.

To the *third* passage, which is from the epistle to the Colossians, I say there the Apostle condemns the heresy of Simon Magus, who, following the Platonists, taught that certain angels must be adored as lesser gods who made the world and spoke through the prophets, and that no one could please the supreme God who is invisible except through these angels. See what Irenaeus says about this heresy (1, 20), as well as Tertullian (*de Praescriptione*) and Epiphanius (*Panarion, in haeresi Simonis*). On this idolatry, or magic, wherein all the interpreters of this passage explain the angels were adored in place of God, or Christ. St. John Chrysostom (*hom. 7 in epist. ad Coloss.*) says, "There are several who say it is not fitting to be reconciled

Ch. XX: The Opposing Arguments Are Answered

through Christ and go to the Father, but through the angels. This is why [Paul] treated left and right on what has been done by Christ." So also Oecumenius and Theophylactus explain it; Ambrose on this passage thinks it is those who worship the stars.

Jerome (*quest. 10 ad Algasiam*) and Haymo teach on this passage that those who make sacrifice to angels must be rebuked, nor does Theodoret dissent from them, nay more he clearly teaches that here the followers of Simon are observed, who said God cannot be embraced except by pleasing the angels, and from that very Council, which he cites, it appears it was idolatry which Paul rebuked. Thus the Council of Laodicea says (Canon 35), "Christians must not forsake the Church of God and go away to invoke the angels and gather assemblies, for such things are forbidden. If, therefore, any one shall be found engaged in this covert idolatry, let him be anathema, for he has forsaken our Lord Jesus Christ, the Son of God, and has gone over to idolatry." Where, as you see, the Council does not condemn any veneration you like of the angels, but that which is proper to God.

But what Theodoret says about the oratories of St. Michael can be understood in two ways. *a)* That he meant to say the heretics built oratories to St. Michael so that when they worshipped there according to the heresy of Simon, by sacrificing to them, etc.; *b)* That he meant to say the temples constructed by the heretics to sacrifice to wicked angels were turned by Catholics into oratories of St. Michael, and from the multitude of such places it is gathered how much the heresy of Simon once ran riot there.

The fact that temples of idols were once converted into basilicas of the martyrs and other saints is certain from

Theodoret himself (*de Martyribus*, lib. 8) and still at Rome the temple of all the gods is seen converted into the Church of all Saints, and the temple of Castor and Pollux into the Church of Ss. Cosmos and Damian. St. Gregory (*Dialogues*, 2, 8) writes that a temple of Apollo was turned into an oratory of St. Martin, and St. Gregory himself (*Lib. Epist.* 19, 71 *ad Mellitum*), commanded Augustine, the bishop of England, not to destroy the temples of idols, but to sprinkle them with holy water and adorn them with the relics of the saints, so that at length they would convert them into temples of the true God.

3) The *third* argument. The saints that are dead now are not aware of the prayers of the living, therefore they are invoked in vain. That the Saints are not aware of the prayers of the living is proven by argumentation. *a)* Scripture attributes the searching of hearts and to know the thoughts of men to God alone, "You alone know the heart of all the children of men" (3 Kings 8:39). *b)* Job 14:21, "Whether his children shall be noble or ignoble, he shall not understand." *c)* Ecclesiastes 9:5, where it is said: "The living know they are going to die, but the dead know nothing further." *d)* In Isaiah 63:16 it is said, "For you are our father and Abraham did not know us, and Israel has been ignorant of us." *e)* 4 Kings 22:20, God said to king Josiah, "I will gather you to your fathers, and you will be gathered to your tomb in peace, that your eyes may not see all the evils which I will bring in upon this place." *f)* St. Augustine (*On the care for the dead*, 13), says, "Then if our parents have forsaken us, how do they take part in our cares and affairs? But if parents do not, who else is there among the dead who should know what we are doing, or what we suffer? Isaiah the Prophet says, 'For you are our Father: because Abraham hath not known us, and Israel is

Ch. XX: The Opposing Arguments Are Answered

not cognizant of us'." If such patriarchs were unaware of something done to the people begotten from them, how do the dead mix in the knowledge of the deeds and acts of the living and help them?

Likewise, Gregory Nazianzen (*Oratio in Gorgoniam sororem suam*) says, "And if you take any account of our affairs, and holy souls receive from God this privilege, do accept these words of mine, in place of, and in preference to many panegyrics." Certainly you see Gregory was uncertain as to whether the saints know our prayers. We read such uncertainty in St. Augustine (*de Vera Religione*, 55), when he says, "If any angel or man loves God, I am certain that he will also love me; whoever remains in him can also sense human prayers, in him he hears me."

We read a similar doubt in Origen (*in epist. ad Romanos*, lib. 2), not far from the beginning: "If the saints that have already left the body and are with Christ do anything and labor for us, in like manner as the angels do who are employed in the ministry of our salvation; or again, even sinners themselves that have left the body, do something proposed to their mind by the angels, let this also remain among the hidden things of God, and the mysteries that are not to be committed unto writing."

I respond: The consequent of this argument is neither good nor true, because it is assumed. Therefore, the first consequent can be denied since it is certain from so many testimonies of the Fathers and so many miracles shown by God, that those who invoke the saints are heard and obtain what they seek. Certainly the saints are not invoked in vain, even if, at length, they do not hear nor are cognizant of our prayers, for someone else does in their place, just as one does not entreat a king when he knows for a fact that the king is not going to read his supplication, but someone else from his hall, and just the same, so obtains what he asks, as if the king had read his entreaty.

Thereupon, what is assumed is not true, that the saints do not know what we ask of them. Even if there were an uncertainty, just the same they know what is absent and the things we mention by the affect of the heart alone. Nevertheless, it is certain they are cognizant, seeing that we showed that they are present to us and have charge of our affairs. And certainly, the argument: *The saints are rightly invoked, therefore they know what we ask*, has a better consequent than: *They do not know what we ask, therefore they are not rightly invoked.* The antecedent of the first argument stands from the consensus of the whole Church; the antecedent of the second is not proved by any solid foundation.

Furthermore, on the mode whereby they are cognizant, there are four teachings of the doctors. Some say they are cognizant from the relation of the angels, who both ascend to heaven and come down to us from there. St. Augustine approves of this reasoning (*de cura pro mortuis*, c. 15).

Others say the souls of the saints, just like the angels, by a marvelous speed of nature are everywhere and hear the prayers of supplicants themselves. St. Jerome seems to hold this reasoning (*Contra Vigilantium*). But neither is sufficient, for neither the angels, nor the souls of the saints, even if they are present, can naturally recognize our prayers when we pray merely in thought. And besides, to be cognizant of the prayers which are made at the same time in very different places, speed does not suffice, rather, true ubiquity is required, which we believe neither angels nor the souls of men are suited to have.

Others say the saints see in God all things from the very principle of beatitude, which pertains to them in some

Ch. XX: The Opposing Arguments Are Answered

mode, and hence even our prayers directed to them. So St. Gregory teaches (*Moral.* 12, 13), and St. Thomas (*III*, q. 10 art. 2; *II-IIæ* q. 83, art. 4) and Cajetan (commenting on the same citation of Thomas), and this is a probable opinion.

Lastly, others say the saints do not see in the Word our prayers from the principle of their beatitude, but merely our prayers as God reveals them at the time when we pour them fourth. In this way the prophets were cognizant of future events while God revealed such to them, and many of the saints here on earth had a gift from God whereby they were cognizant of human thoughts and even the most secret deeds, such as Samuel (1 Kings 9), Elijah (4 Kings 5), Peter (Acts 5) and St. Benedict, as St. Gregory writes (*Dialogues*, 2, 29). And we read the same thing about St. Bernard, Francis, and many others. How much more is it to be believed that the saints in heaven possess this gift? This is the clear teaching of St. Augustine in *Care for the dead*, chapter 15.

From these last two opinions, the first one is simply more probable, because if the saints were to need new revelation, the Church would not so boldly say to all the saints, "pray for us", but would at some point ask from God that he would reveal our prayers to them. Then, we could not so easily explain why the saints must now be invoked and were not invoked before the coming of Christ. Nevertheless, the second of these last two opinions is more suitable to convince the heretics, for the Calvinists do not receive higher reasoning. Since they think the saints do not see God before the day of judgment, they cannot reject this opinion, for even if the saints do not see God, still our prayers could be revealed to them just as if they were here on earth.

St. Robert Bellarmine

Now, someone will say, how will we answer the heretics according to this last opinion if they should ask why the prayers of the living were not revealed to the fathers in limbo, if they are now revealed in heaven?

I respond: The reason why we argue here that they were not ordinarily revealed to the fathers in limbo is that they were not yet blessed. For, it pertains to perfect beatitude to know these things, which pertain to themselves, and especially what they do to honor and glory. Besides, the saints in limbo did not have charge of our affairs in this way, nor were they placed over the Church, as the saints in heaven are, as we showed above and we manifestly deduced from Sacred Scripture.

Thus we will answer the arguments from Scripture. *a)* I say to the *first*, only God knows all the thoughts of all hearts, and naturally by his own power; but the saints only know those things which God manifests to them, whether in the beatific vision or even by a new revelation.

b) St. Gregory answers the *second* (*Moral.* 12, 13), when he explains this passage. St. Job meant to say that naturally the dead are not cognizant of what the living do, still the saints, who enjoy the glory of God, see everything that pertains to them in God.

c) The answer to the *third* is the same.

d) To the *fourth*, St. Jerome explains the "knowledge" involved in this passage in regard to approbation, that the sense is: "Abraham knew us not, *i.e.* he does not have us for sons, and does not love us, but scorns us, because he knows we have receded from you," and this seems the literal exposition. Nevertheless, because St. Augustine (*On the care of the dead*, 13) explains this on knowledge properly so called, therefore, the response can also be made that Abraham and Israel (Jacob) and other fathers of

Ch. XX: The Opposing Arguments Are Answered

the Old Testament did not know their living posterity because they were not yet blessed, and naturally the dead do not know what the living do.

e) To the *fifth*, the answer is the same.

f) I say to the *sixth*, in that chapter, Augustine speaks about cognition and natural conversation. He only contends that the dead do not live with us, and are not solicitous for our affairs, nor do they know them as they did when they lived here. For what they know naturally by divine revelation, which is the question here, he clearly teaches (*ibid.*, 15). And that they can come here by divine power and bring us aid, he also teaches (*ibid.* 19), when he says: "We are not to think then, that to be interested in the affairs of the living is in the power of any departed souls you like, only because the Martyrs are present to heal or help some men. Rather, we are to understand that it must needs be by a Divine power that the Martyrs are interested in affairs of the living, from the very fact that for the departed to be by their proper nature interested in affairs of the living is impossible."

Now, someone will say, Augustine thought his mother was blessed, as he himself says (*On the Care of the dead*, 16), and still in the same place he proves the dead do not know what we do, because his mother never came to console him.

I respond: The saints know our prayers and can come when they will; just the same, on that account they know all of our affairs but are not continually present in our affairs in the way that men are, as Augustine teaches in that citation with the example of his mother.

To the passage of Nazianzen I say that the conjunction "if" that he uses is not of a man in doubt, but one affirming, as when the Apostle says to Philemon, "If you have me as a friend, take him." For Gregory Nazianzen asserts throughout his works that the Saints see what is done here. In his oration on Athanasius, he says, "I know it is a fact that you look upon our affairs from on high and extend a hand to those who labor for good, and the greater he works the more he is freed from his bonds."

To the other passage of St. Augustine I say, he most rightly says, "Whoever remains in it, and can hear human prayers," because many remain in God who cannot hear human prayers, namely all those who are in charity and still are not yet blessed, for all who remain in charity remain in God (1 John 4:16). Nevertheless, not everyone who remains in charity is now blessed in heaven.

To the passage of Origen, I say that there he argues on the natural conversation and knowledge seeing that he is not ambiguous as to whether the saints see what we do, and help us with their prayers, which he teaches in clear words (*Contra Celsum*, lib. 8 and *homil. 26* on the book of Numbers; *hom. 16 in Josue*, and other places). Rather, he only argues whether the holy spirits of men are just like angels and demons, which truly are always present, the former to do good and the latter strive in earnest to drag us to evil with them.

4) The *fourth* argument. God, is most prepared to hear us, and loves us more than any of the saints, therefore the saints are invoked in vain. Indeed, it is a sign of unbelief to invoke the saints, for the Lord says, "Ask and you will receive," (Luke 11:9) and "If you will ask anything of the Father in my name, he will give it to you" (John 16:23). And St. Paul says, "Let us go with confidence to the throne of grace" (Hebrews 4:16). Besides, St. John Chrysostom (*hom. de profectu Evangelii*, tom. 3) says, "It is certain that you do not need a patron with God, nor much speaking to charm

Ch. XX: The Opposing Arguments Are Answered

others. Although you are alone, and you lack a patron, and pray to God by yourself, still you will be altogether suited to pray, and God will not easily agree when others pray for us, as when we ourselves pray, even if we are full of a great number of evils." He says the same thing in his preface to Psalm 4.

I respond: Nothing can be gathered from this argument other than that we would seek the prayers of the living in vain and from a lack of faith. Besides, although God is prepared to hear, and loves us more than any saint, still he is prepared to hear the saints more than us, and he loves the saints more than us. Prayer, to obtain something, requires a disposition in the one making the prayer which we do not always have. Thus, it is more useful that we go to God with the saints than alone. This is why God says, "Go to my servant Job so that he will pray for you" (Job 42:8). And in Genesis 20:17, Abimelech could not be healed except by the prayers of Abraham. In Ezechiel 20:46, God himself asked a man to oppose his wrath, seeing that he wanted to forgive the people, but through the prayers of some holy man. Lastly, who does not know that the prayers of the saints assist predestination itself, because God so determined to obtain the salvation of some man by the prayers of the saints?

Now, to the passages of Scripture I say, it is impertinence, for when we pray to the saints, it is not the case that then we ask nothing of God, or that we do not seek him with faith; nay more it is the contrary. We implore the prayers of the saints to be able to come to God with greater trust, and more easily obtain what we ask.

To the passage of Chrysostom, I say in the first place, he speaks on those who implore the prayers of mortals, not of those who invoke the saints reigning with Christ, as is clear from these very words: "You do not need ... much speaking to charm others." I say besides, he rebukes those who do not pray themselves, but only ask the prayers of others, as many rich men do when they refuse to labor in prayer, and for that reason only bestow alms on the poor so that the latter would pray for them. He rightly places those who pray for themselves before them, even if they cannot have the prayer of others. Nevertheless, those who both pray for themselves and at the same time implore the prayers of others must be placed before both types of men, as we see from Chrysostom himself in many citations, such as in *Homily 5 on Matthew*, "Let us not then be looking open-mouthed towards others, and being idle depend on the merits of others. For it is true, the prayers of the saints have the greatest power; on condition however of our repentance and amendment." And in *Homily 1 on 1 Thessalonians*, he says, "And what need, you say, have I of another's prayer, if I am on the alert myself. And in sooth, do not place yourself in a situation to need it; I do not wish that you should; but we are always in need of it, if we think rightly. ... Knowing these things, therefore, let us neither despise the prayers of the Saints, nor throw everything upon them; that we may not, on the one hand, be indolent and live carelessly; nor on the other deprive ourselves of a great advantage" (see also *Homily 8 in Matthew* and *Homily 43 in Genesis*).

5) The *fifth* argument. Christ taught us in word and example who must be invoked. For in Matthew 6 and Luke 11, he says, "Praying, say Our Father, who art in heaven," even Christ himself, as often as he addresses the Father, "Father, glorify me," (John 12:28), "Father, the hour has come," (John 17:1) etc. Therefore neither the angels nor

Ch. XX: The Opposing Arguments Are Answered

dead men must be invoked. So the Centuriators gather (*Centur. 1*, 1, 4, column 139).

I respond: The same Centuriators would have it the Lord's prayer is related to the Father alone in the same place. For they hold: "He does not bid an angel or a patriarch or a dead prophet to be invoked, but only the Father." So I ask, is it lawful to invoke the Son and the Holy Spirit, or not? They will answer that it is lawful, since next they teach: "But that the Son may and must also be invoked, examples teach. ... Also that the Holy Spirit may and must be invoked can be gathered from the words of Baptism." Thus the Centuriators. Therefore, it does not conclude the argument; Christ by word and example taught that only the Father is invoked; therefore holy men or angels must not be invoked. For if this would conclude the argument, it would also lead us to the conclusion that Christ taught by word and example that only the Father is invoked, thus, the Son of God and the Holy Spirit must not be invoked. I also add that when Christ taught the apostles to pray, he meant to advise the disciples on what they must ask for, not on whom they are going to pray to. It is certain enough that we must pray to God and also God alone when we seek the author of gifts, but on the mode of prayer or on asking for things the apostles are uncertain when they ask in Luke 11:1, "Teach us to pray."

6) The *sixth* argument. There exists no command of Scripture, or example, or promise on the invocation of the Saints; therefore the saints must not be invoked. So the *Augsburg Confession* surmises (art. 12) and all others who normally use this argument.

I respond: If this argument would conclude the matter, it would also cause the saints not to pray for the Church, either in general, or in particular, which the *Apologia for the Augsburg Confession* clearly concedes. For so it says: "On the saints, even if we concede that they pray for the universal Church in general for the living, so in heaven they pray for the Church in general, even if there is no testimony on dead men praying that is extant in Scripture, apart from that dream taken from the second book of the Maccabees." Thus the *Apologia*. Then, for what attains to a command, certainly no command is required when necessity itself impels us. There are a great many examples in both the Old Testament and the New, as we showed above. Then, as for promise, they are hardly in want, since innumerable signs and prodigies that took place provide a witness for the invocation of the saints, God hears those who apply the patronage of the saints to obtain something from God. Nevertheless, in Job 42:8, we have a particular command, example and promise; from which a judgment can be made in regard to the whole nature of invocation: "Go to my servant Job." Lo! A command! "And he will pray for you." Lo! An example! "His face I will receive, that the foolishness will not be imputed to you." Lo! A promise.

But they will say that Job was alive and present, whereas the saints are dead and absent. But it is not so; for the saints, on their side, are now especially alive, whereby they hear prayers and can go before God for their suppliants. Nor are they absent in regard to favorable answer to prayer, although they seem absent from a place, as we sufficiently proved above. And it is certain in regard to the angels from what we read in Psalm 137 [138]:1, "In the sight of the angels I will sing to you." And in 1 Corinthians 4, "We are made a spectacle to the world, before angels and men." Likewise, in regard to holy men, it is clear from Apocalypse 11:18 and 19:8, where the saints are described in heaven seeing those things which are

Ch. XX: The Opposing Arguments Are Answered

done on earth. For this reason St. Basil, in his work *On Virginity*, says, "Reverence that spouse who is everywhere with the Father and the Holy Spirit, accompanied with innumerable multitudes of angels and souls of holy fathers. For there is not one of them who does not see all things everywhere." St. Gregory the Great (*Moral.* 12, 12) says, "Concerning holy souls, since they behold the brightness of Almighty God within, we cannot for a moment suppose that there is any thing outside that they know not."

7) The *seventh* argument. No man dares act the part of an advocate[1] with an earthly prince unless he has been admitted by the prince himself. Thus Calvin says, "From where do the worms find such a license that they force in patrons when it is not read that the office was enjoined upon them?"

I respond: We do not make saints advocates or patrons of this kind, of the sort that here on earth act in judicial matters and defend cases, who do not seek mercy but justice. It is necessary for advocates of this sort to be admitted by the magistrate. On the other hand, we attribute to the saints only that office which here on earth we usually attribute to friends and familiars of princes, who often intercede for poor wretches, nor do they need any new authority to do that.

8) The *eighth* argument. Many are invoked who are not only not saints, but also didn't even exist, such as Christopher, George, Catherine, etc. Therefore invocation is superstitious. So Melanchthon reasons in his *Apologia for the Augsburg Confession*, art. 21, and Calvin in his book

---

[1] Translator's note: The word in the Latin here is *causidicus*, which refers to an attorney that acts on someone's behalf and constituted as such by a court.

St. Robert Bellarmine

On a plan of true reformation of the Church, where, with his customary modesty, he calls St. Dominic an executioner, St. Medard and certain others beasts, while he generally calls the saints monsters.

I respond: There are indeed apocryphal and uncertain histories of certain saints. Nevertheless, it is not for that reason that those saints never existed. For, if one were permitted to so argue, then most of the apostles could not be numbered among the saints. Their histories, which are related either by Abdia or others, are for the most part not altogether beyond doubt. Indeed, we have in the Gospel the calling of the apostles and a few scanty details of their lives, but not the happy sleep of St. James the Greater (Acts 12:2) and the glorious death which the Lord predicts for St. Peter (John 21:18-19). But of the other apostles, we do not have any information on their end in the Scriptures. For that reason Pope Gelasius (*Can. Sancta Romana*, dist. 15) numbers the history of St. George among the apocryphal histories, and yet affirms that George himself must be venerated, because even if the history then extant was apocryphal, still those apocryphal stories would not be a universal custom of the Church, whereas the memory of George, Christopher and Catherine was most honored.

Add to this that if the histories of three or four saints are apocryphal, the histories of innumerable others are certain and beyond doubt; even the sanctity and glory of certain ones are preached in Scripture, such as the Blessed Virgin Mary, John the Baptist, Peter, Stephen and others. Wherefore, if our adversaries refuse to venerate George, Christopher or Catherine, what about the uncertain histories of others, why do they not venerate Mary, John, Stephen, Peter, James, whose histories they cannot deny? Why also do they place men in their calendars, who were

Ch. XX: The Opposing Arguments Are Answered

the worst sort of men, whom they are also compelled to admit are of a different religion than themselves, if they would attend to the matter a little more diligently (see the sixth dialogue of the Englishman Alan Copus).

9) The *ninth* argument. If the invocation of the saints lacked superstition and imitation of paganism, certainly they would not seek one thing from a saint and something else from another when God is the one author of all gifts, and he can equally concede whatever one likes through the intercession of one and through the intercession of another. But Catholics invoke one against plague, another against a pain of the eyes, and another against a pain of the teeth.

I respond: The Centuriators drive home this argument, as well as Calvin and others. But they are merely renewing an ancient complaint of Julian the Apostate (cited by Cyril in *Julianum*, lib. 6), of the Manicheans (cited by Augustine, *contra Faustum*, 3, 4) and of Vigilantius (cited by Jerome, *in Vigilantium*). For they all complained that we turned idols into martyrs and worship them with the same votive offerings, which is really an argument that our fathers are Cyril, Augustine, Jerome and the rest of the Church which communicated with them, whereas the fathers of Calvin and the Centuriators are Julian the Apostate, Faustus, the Manicheans, Vigilantius, and the other apostates or heretics who communicated with them.

But that I might approach the matter more properly, I say, God can, if he willed, concede everything through whatever saint you like, and without the saints he gives many things, or everything. Sometimes he wills to work some miracle by the intercession of one, or something else by the intercession of another. Yet, who knows the counsel of God? Or who can say to him, why do you act in this way? Just as God also works many miracles through one, and through another, perhaps a greater through none, he alone knows the reason for this, as St. Augustine teaches (*epist. 137 to the clergy and people of Hippo*), "God is everywhere, it is true, and He that made all things is not contained or confined to dwell in any place; and He is to be worshipped in spirit and in truth by His true worshipers, in order that, as He hears in secret, He may also in secret justify and reward. But in regard to the answers to prayer which are visible to men, who can search out His reasons for appointing some places rather than others to be the scene of miraculous interpositions? To many the holiness of the place in which the body of the blessed Felix is buried is well known, and to this place I desired them to repair; because from it we may receive more easily and more reliably a written account of whatever may be discovered in either of them by divine interposition. For I myself knew how, at Milan, at the tomb of the saints, where demons are brought in a most marvelous and awful manner to confess their deeds, a thief who had come thither intending to deceive by perjuring himself was compelled to acknowledge his own theft, and to restore what he had taken away; and is not Africa also full of the bodies of holy martyrs? Yet we do not know of such things being done in any place here. Even as the gift of healing and the gift of discerning of spirits are not given to all saints? As the apostle declares; so it is not at all the tombs of the saints that it has pleased Him who divides to each severally as He will, to cause such miracles to be wrought." He adds to these, that even if some saints sometimes shine more with some kind of miracle than others, nevertheless, we seek everything from all, nor do we think we should so seek

Ch. XX: The Opposing Arguments Are Answered

from one that we may not also suppose it can be obtained by the intercession of another.

10) The *tenth* argument. The saints can obtain or merit nothing for themselves in heaven, therefore much less for us.

I respond: The saints cannot merit either for themselves or for others. Nevertheless, from the preceding merits they can obtain both for themselves and for others, that which they seek in prayer; for they seek for themselves the glory of the body, but for us all things for which we are in need.

But one might object, they have already received the reward for their merits, therefore nothing further is due to them.

I respond: They indeed received the reward but this also pertains to their reward, that they will always be friends of God and as friends, they obtain from God whatever they seek. Just as even here on earth, if someone who fought for a long time for a king, and he received all of his wages, still, he will be able to make supplication for others and by the right of friendship will obtain much more easily than another who never served the king.

Finis